EDITED BY:
SHALVA WEIL
CONSUELO CORRADI
MARCELINE NAUDI

D1216673

FEMICIDE ACROSS EUROPE

Theory, research and prevention

POLICY PRESS SHORTS POLICY & PRACTICE

First published in Great Britain in 2018 by

Policy Press
University of Bristol
1-9 Old Park Hill
Bristol
BS2 8BB
UK
t: +44 (0)117 954 5940
pp-info@bristol.ac.uk
www.policypress.co.uk

North America office:
Policy Press
c/o The University of Chicago Press
1427 East 60th Street
Chicago, IL 60637, USA
t: +1 773 702 7700
f: +1 773 702 9756
sales@press.uchicago.edu
www.press.uchicago.edu

British Library Cataloguing in Publication Data
A catalogue record for this book is available from the British Library.

Library of Congress Cataloging-in-Publication Data
A catalog record for this book has been requested.

ISBN 978-1-4473-4713-2 (paperback)
ISBN 978-1-4473-4714-9 (ePub)
ISBN 978-1-4473-4715-6 (Mobi)
ISBN 978-1-4473-4716-3 (OA PDF)

Cover design by Policy Press
Front cover: image kindly supplied by Alamy
Printed and bound in Great Britain by CMP, Poole
Policy Press uses environmentally responsible print partners

This book pays tribute to the thousands upon thousands of women who are killed unnecessarily each year.

This publication is based upon work from COST Action IS1206 supported by COST (European Cooperation in Science and Technology).

COST (European Cooperation in Science and Technology) is a funding agency for research and innovation networks. Our Actions help connect research initiatives across Europe and enable scientists to grow their ideas by sharing them with their peers. This boosts their research, career and innovation.
http://www.cost.eu

Funded by the Horizon 2020 Framework Programme of the European Union.

Contents

Figures and tables

Figures

Tables

Acknowledgements

The following persons were part of the COST Action IS1206, 'Femicide across Europe'. Our deepest thanks are extended to them.

MC Chair

Prof Shalva Weil, Hebrew University of Jerusalem, Israel

Belgium

Dr David Berliner, Universite Libre de Bruxelles
Dr David Paternotte, Universite libre de Bruxelles
Dr Annalisa Casini, Universite Catholique de Louvain

Bosnia and Herzegovina

Dr Lisa Muftic, University of Sarajevo Zmaja od Bosne

Croatia

Dr Ivana Radacic, Ivo Pilar Institute of Social Sciences
Dr Irena Cajner Mraovic, University of Zagreb

Cyprus

Dr Christiana Kouta, Cyprus University of Technology
Dr Elena Rousou, Cyprus University of Technology

Denmark

Dr Yvonne Morck, Roskilde University

Estonia

Dr Marion Pajumets, Institute of International and Social Studies
Mr Jako Salla, Tallinn University

Finland

Dr Riikka Kotanen, University of Helsinki

France

Dr Lisa Anteby-Yemini, CNRS, IDEMEC-AIX Marseille University
Ms Valerie Raffin, French Ministry of Higher Education, Research and Innovation

Georgia

Prof Tina (Tiko) Tsomaia, Georgian Institute of Public Affairs

Germany

Dr Monika Schrottle, Arbeitsstelle Gender Studies
Prof Ruth Seifert, University of Applied Sciences, Regensburg
Ms Ksenia Meshkova, Humboldt University of Berlin
Prof Clarissa Rudolph, University of Applied Sciences Regensburg

Greece

Dr Athena Peglidou, University of Aegean
Dr Joanna Tsiganou, National Centre for Social Research

ACKNOWLEDGEMENTS

Dr Katerina Vasilikou, Academy of Athens
Ms Stamatia Papagiannopoulou

Iceland

Dr Freydis Freysteinsdottir, University of Iceland
Ms Halldora Gunnarsdottir, City of Reykjavik
Ms Ingibjorg Thordardottir

Ireland

Ms Siobán O'Brien Green, Trinity College Dublin

Israel

Dr Yifat Bitton, The College of Management Academic Studies
Prof Revital Shayovitz, The Institute of Criminology
Dr Anita Nudelman, Ben Gurion University
Dr Esther Serok, Hebrew University of Jerusalem
Dr Hava Dayan, University of Haifa
Ms Amal A. Najammy, Ben Gurion University

Italy

Prof Consuelo Corradi, Lumsa University
Prof Augusto Gnisci, University of Campania 'Luigi Vanvitell'"
Prof Anna Costanza Baldry, Seconda Universita degli Studi di
Napoli

Latvia

Dr Andrejs Judins, Centre for Public Policy

Lithuania

Dr Vilana Pilinkaite Sotirovic, Lithuanian Social Research Centre
Dr Vita Kontvaine (Petrusauskaite), Lithuanian Social Research Centre

Malta

Dr Marceline Naudi, University of Malta
Ms Katya Unah, Ministry for European Affairs and Equality
Ms Christine Marchand-Agius, Foundation for Social Welfare Services

Netherlands

Dr Marieke Liem, Universiteit Leiden

Norway

Prof Anne Ryen, University of Agder

Poland

Dr Magdalena Grzyb, Jagiellonian University, Krakow
Dr Tomasz Kozlowski, Mikolaj Kopernik University, Torun

Portugal

Prof Maria Jose Magalhaes, Universidade do Porto, CIEG/ ISCSP
Prof Conceicao Nogueira, Centro de Psicologia da Universidade do Porto
Prof Sofia Neves, Instituto Universitario da Maia

Romania

Dr Ecaterina Georgeta Balica, Institute of Sociology
Dr Valentina Marinescu, University of Bucharest
Dr Anca Adriana Cusmir, Institute of Sociology
Dr Silvia Branea, University of Bucharest
Dr Raluca Nicoleta Simion, Institute of Sociology
Mr Radu-Emilian Gavris, DGPMB

Serbia

Prof Vesna Nikolic-Ristanovic, University of Belgrade
Dr Sanja Copic, Institute of Criminological and Sociological
Research
Ms Ljiljana Stevkovic, University of Belgrade

Slovenia

Prof Milica Antic, University of Ljubljana
Ms Jasna Podreka, University of Ljubljana
Ms Darja Tadic, University of Ljubljana
Ms Nina Perger, University of Ljubljana

Spain

Dr Santiago Jose Boira Sarto, Universidad de Zaragoza
Dr Chaime Marcuello, Universidad de Zaragoza
Prof Yolanda Rodriguez Castro, University of Vigo
Prof Maria Lameiras Fernandez, University of Vigo
Dr Laura Otero Garcia, National Institute Carlos III
Dr Belen Sanz Barbero, National Institute Carlos III
Dr Carmen Vives Cases, University of Alicante
Dr Isabel Goicolea Julian, Universidad de Alicante

Sweden

Dr Lucas Gottzen, Linkoping University
Dr Sofia Strid, Orebro University
Dr Viveka Enander, University of Gothenburg

Turkey

Dr Sadik Toprak, Bülent Ecevit University
Dr Sümeyra Buran, Medeniyet University

United Kingdom

Dr Heidi Stoeckl, London School of Hygiene and Tropical
Medicine
Dr Giorgia Dona, University of East London
Dr Aisha K. Gill, University of Roehampton
Ms Hilary Fisher
Dr Jacqueline Sebire, Bedfordshire Police Service

FYR Macedonia

Assoc Prof Biljana Chavkoska, International Balkan University
Dr Viktorija Chavkoska, Ministry of Foreign Affairs

COST Science Officer

Dr Rossella Magli, COST Association

Grant-Holder Administrator

Mr Aristodimos Lanitis, Cyprus University of Technology

Notes on editors

Shalva Weil is Senior Researcher at the Research Institute for Innovation in Education at the Hebrew University of Jerusalem, Israel, and Research Fellow in the Department of Biblical and Ancient Studies at UNISA, University of South Africa. From 2013 to 2017 she served as Chair of the Cost Action IS1206 on 'Femicide across Europe'. She has addressed the Parliaments of Portugal, Aragon (Spain) and Rome, and spoken at three UN meetings on femicide. She runs an empowerment programme for slum migrant women of Caucasian origin and has researched intimate partner femicide among Ethiopian immigrants in Israel. She has published over 100 journal articles, including 10 in scientific journals on femicide, and edited special issues on femicide and several books on other subjects.

Consuelo Corradi is Professor of Sociology and Vice-Chair for Research and International Relations at Lumsa University, Rome, Italy. She served as Co-Chair of the Cost Action IS1206 on 'Femicide across Europe'. Her research interests include violence against women, femicide and, more recently, the cross-national comparison of gender policy regimes across Europe. Her most recent book is *The concept and measurement of violence against women and men* (Policy Press, 2017), co-authored with Sylvia Walby and others. Consuelo was Vice-President of the European Sociological Association from 2007 to 2009.

Marceline Naudi is a social worker by profession and a Senior Lecturer within the Department of Gender Studies at the University of Malta. She teaches and supervises student research on gender issues, violence against women and other anti-oppressive issues. She is active on the issues of gender equality and violence against women, LGBTIQ, as well as wider human rights issues in Malta and throughout Europe. She is currently a board member of the Women Against Violence Europe (WAVE) network, and Vice President of GREVIO, the Council of Europe monitoring body of the Istanbul Convention. She has headed the European Observatory on Femicide since January 2018.

ONE

Research and prevention of femicide across Europe

Shalva Weil

Introduction

Femicide is the intentional killing of women and girls because of their gender. Femicides are usually perpetrated by intimate partners (for example, husbands or boyfriends) or family members (for example, fathers, brothers or cousins), who are usually familiar males; on rare occasions the perpetrators can be women, either lesbian partners or kin. A global study of homicides carried out by the United Nations Office on Drugs and Crime (UNODC) in 2012 showed that 79% of all homicide victims were male. The global average male homicide rate was, at 9.7 per 100,000, almost four times the global average female rate. However, the majority of homicides in the domestic field were femicides (which the authors called 'female intentional homicides') perpetrated by intimate partners or family members. Of 93,000 global femicides reported in 2012, 43,600 women – that is, nearly 50% – were killed by intimate partners or family members, as opposed to only 6% among male homicides (UNODC, 2014: 53).

Although the killing of women has been rampant in Europe for generations and generations, to the best of our knowledge, this is the first book on femicide across Europe. It has been written by a team of interdisciplinary scholars from different European countries, united in the desire to bring awareness to the phenomenon and thereby eliminate it. It examines comparative quantitative and qualitative data collection, and the impact of culture and prevention programmes aimed at combatting femicide. The subject has become particularly pertinent with the influx of migrants to Europe; although to date it has not been proven that there are more femicide incidents among the migrants than among the more established populations.

While femicide has not been totally ignored in the past, until now, the designation has had various gender-neutral or even male-centred meanings, such as 'lethal killings of women', 'female homicide', 'female homicide victimization' or even 'manslaughter'; meanwhile related topics, such as domestic violence and intimate partner violence, have been studied while ignoring femicide per se. Thus it was that femicide was included in the category 'homicide', while specific forms of femicide were called 'honour killings', 'wife murders' or 'uxoricide'. So long as femicide was regarded as an extreme form of domestic violence, the special gender-related features of this social, gendered phenomenon were obscured. Femicide was 'invisible' and it had to be made 'visible' (Weil, 2016).

A concerted European action

The legitimacy of regarding femicide as a separate social phenomenon changed in 2013 when the authors of the chapters in this book, and many other people listed in it, collaborated on a four-year project initiated by this author and a group of colleagues. It was funded by an intergovernmental framework, COST (Cooperation in Science and Technology), in association with the European Union, and called COST Action IS1206, 'Femicide across Europe'.[1] Until the establishment of this COST Action, European agencies had never recognized the specific act of femicide, although they had funded initiatives on gender issues and violence.

The COST Action on Femicide across Europe, which began in April 2013 and terminated in April 2017, had several aims (Weil, 2015a):

- to produce an articulated and common theoretical and interdisciplinary framework about femicide through the exchange of ideas by researchers, by means of coordinated network meetings, workshops and conferences;
- to establish preliminary conditions for comparisons of European data on femicide, both qualitative and quantitative, in an attempt to reach the level of other countries, which have been more advanced in the study of this subject;
- to set up coalitions on the prevention of femicide across Europe, bringing together established and early career researchers, women's shelters, police and prison personnel as well as policy makers and advocacy groups;
- to publish academic articles as well as recommendations and guidelines for policy makers;
- to monitor femicide by means of advocacy groups, women's shelters, police and prison personnel through the establishment of a European Observatory on Femicide.

---

[1] Until 2014, COST activities were run under the European Commission's FP7, but then the COST Association was set up as an international non-profit association under Belgian law (AISBL). This law integrates governance with the scientific, technical and administrative functions of COST, formerly managed by the European Science Foundation through the COST Office.

In order to achieve its objectives, the Action set up four European working groups: definitions, data collection, cultural issues, and advocacy and prevention. In July 2015 the Action held the first ever training school on femicide in Rome, Italy. Thirty doctoral and postdoctoral students received a stipend to attend, which covered flight and accommodation at the Rome police headquarters. Throughout the five-day school, early-career trainees were mentored by trainers and policy makers in how to prevent femicide; they interacted with advocates, law enforcement agencies, academics and policy makers. Members of the Action networked at annual conferences on femicide in different European cities, such as Lisbon in Portugal (in 2014), Zaragoza in Spain (in 2015) and Ljubljana in Slovenia (in 2016); a final conference was held in Valletta in Malta (in 2017). All the COST meetings took place within Europe, with an attempt to convene conferences and working group meetings in what were described as 'inclusiveness countries',[2] but keynote speakers and invited guests came from India, the US, South Africa and other countries.

The Action also promoted early career students and researchers in short-term scientific missions (STSMs) to travel to different countries (Germany to Sweden, Italy to UK, Greece to Cyprus and so on) to study at host institutions for short periods in order to compare data, and to receive supervision and gain an understanding of the pan-European situation on femicide. In addition, the Action created the first website on global femicide: www.femicide.net

Thirty countries (28 COST Member States, one Cooperating State and one Near Neighbouring Country) signed a Memorandum of Understanding with COST to work on

---

[2]   COST Inclusiveness Target Countries (ITCs) include Bosnia-Herzegovina, Bulgaria, Croatia, Cyprus, Czech Republic, Estonia, Hungary, Latvia, Lithuania, Luxembourg, Republic of Macedonia, Malta, Montenegro, Poland, Portugal, Romania, Republic of Serbia, Slovakia, Slovenia and Turkey.

combating femicide within the framework of the Action IS1206. Each country chose two management committee (MC) members and a number of substitute MC members to attend meetings and network (Weil, 2015b). The nearly 80-strong members and substitute members of the MC, listed at the beginning of this book, met with politicians, legislators and service providers in order to change realities in their own countries and within Europe as a bloc. This effort exemplified that awareness of femicide had grown and that nearly all European countries today acknowledge that it is an important issue.

It is a truism to state that European issues are part of larger global priorities and that Europe is intrinsically connected to world trends. Attempting to combat femicide is not a new phenomenon, but fighting it has been a low international priority. In the absence of clear governmental policies on femicide, women's advocacy groups and nongovernmental, non-profit organizations (NGOs) have worked for years in different countries to prevent manifestations of extreme violence against women. Until recently, most of them focused upon the prevention of domestic violence, but with growing awareness raised by the COST Action, as well as other important organizations, some NGOs are now focusing upon the elimination of femicide in and of itself. The effort is cumulative, and although the focus of this book is Europe, the phenomenon is global.

Final Action dissemination volume

This book effectively summarizes the workings of the COST Action IS1206, 'Femicide across Europe'. The four chapters following this one are parallel to the working groups that the Action set up in Europe. Working Group 1 grappled with the question of definitions of femicide, and indeed, defining femicide can be a challenge. Diana Russell first used the term 'femicide' in 1976 within a broader critical feminist framework during the proceedings of the first International Tribunal on Crimes against Women, in Brussels, Belgium. After the initial impetus, when femicide was defined as a misogynist crime (Radford and Russell, 1992), the designation fell into partial disuse. Meanwhile, the study of femicide evolved and was de facto adapted by international scholars, including Campbell in the US (Campbell et al, 2003), R. and R. Dobash in the UK (Dobash and Dobash, 2015), and Fregoso and Bejarano in Latin America (2013). 'Femicide' was translated into *feminicidio* by the Mexican feminist Lagarde y de los Rios (2008) and used in the Latin American context. Today, however, Latin American scholars use the terms femicide and *feminicidio* interchangeably (Grzyb and Hernandez, 2015), and even Lagarde calls the phenomenon 'femicide' (Lagarde y de los Rios, 2008). Definitional problems are discussed in Chapter 2.

Working Group 2 analysed data collection on femicide in Europe. European countries have databases for homicides, and a few are beginning to disaggregate for femicide too. Chapter 3 reports on the efforts in the working group to compare data collection on femicide from various sources, and to develop recommendations for European countries and organizations on how to improve their femicide data collection.

Working Group 3 focused on culture. Much discussion was placed during the four years of the Action on whether we can talk of 'honour killings' as a type of femicide, and whether 'honour killings' also reflect mainstream culture. In Chapter 4, the authors address the relationship between culture and femicide based on the relevant literature, including an ecological model, in order to determine appropriate ways to treat and prevent femicide,

Working Group 4 was aimed at prevention of femicide. In Chapter 5, the researchers suggest different strategies for prevention, including demanding national obligations to ensure the human rights of women; the enactment of appropriate legal measures to combat the murder of women regardless of their social, economic, ethnic, marriage or sexual status; the development of more efficient and effective fatality reviews and risk assessments; and the creation of holistic educational programmes challenging patriarchal culture.

Chapter 6 represents the culmination of the Action's accomplishments. In this chapter, 26 countries report on their resources, and the authors summarize national attitudes, legal status and programmes instituted to combat femicide. The final chapter in the book both looks back retrospectively to the progress made in the study of femicide in the past few years and looks forward to the establishment of a European Observatory on Femicide (EOF), building on the country reports found in this book.

Global progress

In 2003, the Convention on the Elimination of All Forms of Discrimination against Women presented a broad platform aimed at promoting gender equality. It stated:

'Discrimination against women' shall mean any distinction, exclusion or restriction made on the basis of sex which has the effect or purpose of impairing or nullifying the recognition, enjoyment or exercise by women, irrespective of their marital status, on a basis of equality of men and women, of human rights and fundamental freedoms in the political, economic, social, cultural, civil or any other field.[3]

The convention did not specifically mention violence against women (VAW).

A milestone was achieved in 2011, however, when the Council of Europe Convention on preventing and combating

---

[3] See www.un.org/womenwatch/daw/cedaw/text/econvention.htm

violence against women and domestic violence (henceforth, the Istanbul Convention) was adopted by member states. The convention aimed at protecting women and girls from gender-based violence and men and women from domestic violence (Council of Europe, 2011). According to de Vido, the Istanbul Convention 'must be considered as the most advanced system of protection of women from violence at the international level in force for the time being' (de Vido, 2016–17). While the convention made provisions encompassing criminal justice responses, awareness-raising and social support measures to victims, it is not a treaty and not legally binding for all states (Mc Quigg, 2012). In fact, by 2017, only 22 out of 47 states in the Council of Europe had ratified it. However, it should be clarified that the Istanbul Convention does not deal specifically with the issue of femicide, and the word is not mentioned even once in the document.

In recent years, with much prompting and encouragement from the Academic Council on the United Nations System (ACUNS),[4] the UN's Special Rapporteurs on violence against women, its causes and consequences have taken up the cause of femicide. The previous UN Special Rapporteur, Ms Rashida Manjoo, declared in a report to the Human Rights Council on 23 May 2012, based upon the Report presented by the Expert Group on gender-motivated killing of women: 'gender-related killings are the extreme manifestation of existing forms of violence against women. Such killings are not isolated incidents that arise suddenly and unexpectedly, but are rather the ultimate act of violence which is experienced in a continuum of violence'

---

[4] According to its website: 'ACUNS is a global professional association of educational and research institutions, individual scholars, and practitioners active in the work and study of the United Nations, multilateral relations, global governance, and international cooperation. We promote teaching on these topics, as well as dialogue and mutual understanding across and between academics, practitioners, civil society and students' (http://acuns. org/the-purpose-and-organization-of-acuns).

(Manjoo, 2012: 4–5). Gender-related killing of women is generally understood to refer to the intentional murder of women because they are women, whether they occur in public or in private.

Further progress was made in 2013 when the Vienna Declaration defined femicide as 'the killing of women and girls because of their gender'. It provided a very broad definition of femicide that included female infanticide, gender-based sex selection – known as foeticide – femicide as a result of genital mutilation and femicide related to accusations of witchcraft.

In the United Nations General Assembly on 18 December 2013, Resolution 68/191 noted, albeit in a footnote, that: 'gender-related killing of women and girls was criminalized in some countries as "femicide" or "feminicide" and has been incorporated as such into national legislation in those countries.'[5]

The current Special Rapporteur to the UN, Dr Dubravka Šimonović, who acceded to her position in 2015, called on all states to prevent femicide or the gender-related killing of women (Šimonović, 2017: 5). On 23 September 2016, she presented a report to the General Assembly on 'Modalities for the establishment of femicides/gender-related killings' and recommended setting up 'Femicide Watches' globally. The report proposed disaggregating femicide data from general homicide data, and including intimate partner and family member femicides as well as other forms of femicide (Simonovic, 2017). In May 2017, a prototype of such a 'watch' was presented at the 26th session of the UN Commission on Crime Prevention and Criminal Justice, in Vienna, Austria (UNODC, 2017). In November 2017, Georgia launched its first European Femicide Watch.

---

[5] United Nations Resolution 68/191, on 'Taking action against gender-related killing of women and girls', fn. 1., adopted by the General Assembly at its 70th plenary meeting on 18 December 2013.

Research into femicide in Europe

European countries have databases for homicides, and a few are beginning to disaggregate for femicide too. Eurostat, the European Homicide Monitor (EHM), the European Women's Lobby, the European Institute for Gender Equality (EIGE) and other NGOs are now aware of the need to provide basic and comparable data on femicide. Some European nations already have their own observatories on femicide, for example, Italy (Piacenti and de Pasquali, 2014), the UK (Smith 2016; Women's Aid/Nia 2017), Spain and Portugal. The COST Action invited representatives of these observatories to a meeting in Brussels in 2015 to begin discussions to set up a European Observatory on Femicide (EOF). This led to the coordination of country resources in which 26 European countries summarized their attitudes, legal status and programmes instituted to combat femicide. The challenge of establishing an EOF is now being taken up by Malta.

While Europe had lagged behind the US, Canada, South America and South Africa in research and the study of femicide, European scholars are now at the forefront of publications in the field. Active COST members Corradi, Marcuello, Boira and Weil edited the first special issue on femicide in sociology in a 2016 issue of *Current Sociology* (Marcuello-Servós et al, 2016). Weil and Kouta edited the first special issue in qualitative sociology in a 2017 issue of *Qualitative Sociology Review* (Weil and Kouta, 2017). MC members did not restrict themselves to publications solely in the English language. In 2016, Sofia Neves edited a special issue of the gender studies journal *Ex Aequo* (Neves, 2016), mainly in Portuguese. COST MC members also wrote academic articles reporting on femicide in countries outside Europe, as far afield as Ecuador (Boira et al, 2017) and India (Weil and Mitra vom Berg, 2016). They also published articles in several of the ACUNS volumes on different aspects of femicide, such as femicide among elderly women (Weil, 2017), and European initiatives on femicide (Naudi and Stelmaszek, 2018).

Prevention of femicide in Europe

Increasing awareness of femicide among the general public and in the media could be considered a risk prevention factor, although it has not yet been proven that femicide decreases as awareness increases. As the authors of Chapter 3 show, Eurostat data have shown that while homicides in Europe are decreasing, femicide rates remain the same.

Nevertheless, via reports and articles on the extent and nature of femicide, researchers have impacted prevention programmes. Some COST researchers have initiated and launched a prevention tool (Nudelman et al, 2017). Others are personally involved with law enforcement authorities or with projects aimed at reducing femicide and extreme domestic violence at the grassroots level.

Family or ethnic cultures may be key elements in explaining why different ethnic communities have different forms of femicide (Weil, 2016). In some communities, investigations into femicides have shown that, at least in the case of intimate partner femicide cases, recurrent patterns may emerge. In others, it is usually the case that the victim has suffered years of abuse, either at the hands of members of her natal family or at the hands of her partner. Femicides may be classified according to typical cultural risk factors, depending on the status of the victim, the perpetrator and the attitudes of the community. There are a variety of risk assessment procedures targeted at prevention, which can reduce the risk of femicide actually happening. Different management strategies can then be put in motion, depending on the type of risk.

Conclusions

This chapter has surveyed the relatively short history of the COST Action IS1206, 'Femicide across Europe' (April 2013–April 2017), while acknowledging its interdependence upon international movements and the collaboration and cooperation of different NGOs, some of which were already instrumental in attempting to combat extreme forms of violence against women and girls in different countries or across Europe. This book is one of the outcomes of that Action and reflects the interdisciplinary nature of the study of femicide, alongside the breadth of national experiences of all the authors. Four chapters in the book relate the results of four years of labour in defining what constitutes femicide, in data collection, in assessment of cultural patterns and in the prevention of this form of killing. For the first time, representatives from 30 European states have joined together to report on the state of femicide in their countries. These preliminary reports will form the basis for a European Observatory on Femicide, which may eventually mesh with national Femicide Watches.

Finally, now that the COST Action has terminated, we hope that Europe and the world will vehemently reject the killing of women because of their gender, and will acknowledge that there is no honour whatsoever in committing dishonourable crimes against women and girls. Femicide data has to be collected, analysed and understood in order to prevent more cases of murder of females. European countries must pass laws specifically prohibiting femicides and giving the perpetrators the same or more severe sentences than those for homicides. European parliaments must ratify international guidelines concerning violence against women and femicide, and allocate funding for prevention programmes. Femicide *can* be prevented!

References

Boira, S., Tomas-Aragones, L. and Rivera, N. (2017) 'Intimate partner violence and femicide in Ecuador', *Qualitative Sociology Review* 13(3): 30-47.

Campbell, J. C, Webster, D., Koziol-McLain, J., et al (2003) 'Risk factors for femicide in abusive relationships: results from a multisite case control study', *American Journal of Public Health*, 93(7): 1089–97.

Council of Europe (2011) *Working towards a Convention on preventing and combating violence against women and domestic violence*, https://rm.coe.int/168046031c

de Vido, S. (2017) 'The ratification of the Council of Europe Istanbul Convention by the EU: a step forward in the protection of women from violence in the European legal system', *European Journal of Legal Studies*, 9(2): 69–102.

Dobash, E. R. and Dobash, R. P. (2015) *When men murder women*, Oxford: Oxford University Press.

Fregoso, R.-L. and Bejarano, C. (2013) *Terrorizing women: Feminicide in the Américas*, Durham, NC, and London: Duke University Press.

Grzyb, M. and Hernandez, M. (2015) '"Still a long way ahead": Criminalisation of femicide and addressing impunity in Latin America. Recent developments', in M. Dimitrijevic, A. Filip and M. Platzer (eds) *Femicide. A global issue that demands action. Volume IV*, Vienna: ACUNS, pp 84–93.

Lagarde y de los Rios, M. (2008) 'Antropologia, feminismo y politica: violencia feminicida y derechos humanos de las mujeres', in M. Bullen and C. Diez Mintegui (eds) *Retos teoricos y nuevas practicas*, Ankulegi Antropologia Elkartea, pp 209–39 www.ankulegi.org/wp-content/uploads/2012/03/0008Lagarde.pdf

Manjoo, R. (2012) 'Report of the Special Rapporteur on violence against women, its causes and consequences', A/HRC/20/16, https://www.ohchr.org/Documents/Issues/Women/A.HRC.20.16_En.pdf

Marcuello-Servós, C., Corradi, C., Weil, S. and Boira, S. (2016) 'Femicide: A social challenge', *Current Sociology*, 64(7): 967–74, http://csi.sagepub.com/content/64/7/967.full.pdf+html

McQuigg, R.J.A (2012) 'What potential does the Council of Europe Convention on Violence against Women hold as regards domestic violence?', *International Journal of Human Rights*, 16(7): 947–62.

Naudi, M. and Stelmaszek, B. (2018) 'EU Observatory on Femicide and Other Initiatives in Europe', in H. Hemblade, S. Mobayed, A. Van Uffelen, M. Kirilova, K. Platzer and M. Platzer (eds.) *Femicide IX: Femicide, state accountability and punishment*, Vienna: ACUNS, pp 24–8.

Neves, S. (2016) Special Issue on Femicide. *Ex Aequo*, 34, http://exaequo.apem-estudos.org/revista/revista-ex-aequo-numero-34-2016

Nudelman, A., Boira, S., Tsomaia, T., Balica, E. and Tabagua, S. (2017) 'Hearing their voices: exploring femicide among migrants and culture minorities', *Qualitative Sociology Review*, 10 (3): 49–68.

Piacenti, F. and de Pasquali, P. (2014) 'Femicide in Italy, between the years 2000–2012', *Italian Journal of Criminology* 3, http://www.rassegnaitalianadicriminologia.it/en/home/item/256-il-femminicidio-in-italia-nel-periodo-2000-2012

Simonovic, D. (2017) 'Why we need a femicide watch', in H. Hemblade, A. Filip, A. Hunt, M. Jasser, F. Kainz, M. Gerz, K. Platzer and M. Platzer (eds) *Femicide: Volume VII: Establishing a femicide watch in every country*, Vienna: ACUNS, pp 5–9. www.un.org/ga/search/view_doc.asp?symbol=A/71/398&Submit=Search&Lang=E

Smith, K.I. (2016) 'Counting dead women', https://kareningalasmith.com/counting-dead-women/2015-2

Radford, J. and Russell, D.E.H. (1992) *Femicide. The politics of woman killing*, Twayne, NY: Twayne.

United Nations Office on Drugs and Crime (UNODC) (2014) *Global study on homicide*, Vienna: UNODC, http://www.unodc.org/documents/gsh/pdfs/2014_GLOBAL_HOMICIDE_BOOK_web.pdf.

UNODC (2017) 'Femicide Watch Platform prototype launched at 2017 UN Crime Commission', www.unodc.org/unodc/en/frontpage/2017/May/femicide-watch-platform-prototype-launched-at-2017-un-crime-commission.html?ref=fs4.ohchr.org/Documents/Issues/Women/A.71.398.docx.

Weil, S. (2015a) 'Combatting femicide in multiple ways: the COST Action IS1206 on Femicide across Europe', in A. Filip and M. Platzer (eds) *Femicide: Volume III: Targeting women in conflict*, Vienna: ACUNS, pp 139–41, http://acuns.org/wp-content/uploads/2015/04/Femicide-III_Core-Stanzell.pdf

Weil, S. (2015b) 'Femicide across Europe', in M. Dimitrijevic, A. Filip and M. Platzer (eds) *Femicide: Volume IV: Taking action against gender-related killing of women and girls*, Vienna: ACUNS, pp 118–121, http://fbf7c7e20b173f4d238f-5912a34ad37e49172ffd347ffbe5002d.r41.cf1.rackcdn.com/FemicideVol-IV.pdf

Weil, S. (2016) 'Making femicide visible', *Current Sociology*, Special issue on femicide, 64(7): 1124–37, http://csi.sagepub.com/cgi/reprint/64/7/1124.pdf?ijkey=UTLvgBTPezFfS64&keytype=finite

Weil, S. (2017) 'Femicide of elderly women in Israel', in A. Filip and M. Platzer (eds) *Femicide: Volume VIII: Abuse and femicide of the elderly woman*, Vienna: ACUNS, pp 32–3, http://acuns.org/wp-content/uploads/2017/11/Femicide-Volume-VIII-Abuse-and-Femicide-of-the-Older-Woman.pdf

Weil, S. and Mitra vom Berg, N. (2016) 'Femicide of girls in contemporary India', *Ex Aequo*, 34: 31–43. http://exaequo.apem-estudos.org/artigo/femicide-of-girls-in-contemporary-india

Weil, S. and Kouta, C. (2017) 'Femicide: a glance through qualitative lenses', *Qualitative Sociology Review*, Special issue on 'Researching femicide from a qualitative perspective', 13(3): 6–12, https://search.proquest.com/docview/1966126957?pq-origsite=gscholar

Women's Aid/Nia (2017) 'Femicide census: profiles of women killed by men: redefining an isolated incident', https://1q7dqy2unor827bqjls0c4rn-wpengine.netdna-ssl.com/wp-content/uploads/2017/01/The-Femicide-Census-Jan-2017.pdf

TWO

Femicide definitions

Magdalena Grzyb, Marceline Naudi and Chaime Marcuello-Servós

> The hard sciences are successful because they deal with the soft problems;
>   the soft sciences are struggling because they deal with the hard problems
>   (*Heinz Von Foerster's Theorem Number Two*)

Introduction

Words constrain our perceptions and experiences. Our language builds our thoughts and is a powerful tool to describe the world. The words used in language represent an ambivalent tool that we can use to express our own perceptions, emotions and thoughts, and at the same time, they determine our experiences and social imaginary (cf. Castoriadis, 1975), using a previously established corpus of meanings and order. We can, however, do things and transform the world using language as a tool. Defining a social problem in a certain way leads to a *specific* possible solution, which is dependent on the way the problem is defined. Furthermore, we have to acknowledge that the perspective of those that pose the problem (such as individuals, groups, communities and so on) is affected by their view of the social system within which they perceive the problem (Foerster, 2003).

A central task of the COST Action IS1206 on 'Femicide across Europe' was to clarify and set up a definition of femicide that would be used to talk about this terrible fact: women and girls die, because they are murdered and suffer intentional aggressions leading to their deaths. This fact, which is a social and global human problem, requires significant special attention. It is a scourge that demands action. Where there is a lack of acknowledgement of the problem, there cannot be a clear and convincing political and social solution. However, everything is clear once it is understood. Inside this COST Action, and also outside of this network, it is relevant to grasp the challenge initiated more than four decades ago by Diana E. Russell, who used the term femicide for the first time in 1976, during the first International Tribunal on Crimes against Women. We need to arrive at a consensus to describe this complex, polyhedral and culturally dependent murder (Russell, 2011). A consensual approach facilitates action and joint efforts to describe, report, prevent and eradicate.

In recognition of the debate over the use of the term femicide and the difficulties in establishing a common agreed-upon definition, all the members of the network were given the task of coming up with an agreed definition of femicide and discussing the important issues pertaining to defining femicide. First, we focused on an overview of the history of defining femicide and the subsequent development in the field. Second, we took into consideration distinct femicide types (with attention given to victim–offender relationship, victim and offender characteristics, and event characteristics) and their impact on definitions. And third, we addressed methodological issues pertaining to defining femicide.

Working Group 1 on definitions of femicide, set up by the COST Action, held two exclusive meetings where we invited distinguished researchers as guest speakers on femicide from various corners of the world. The first meeting was held in Jerusalem, Israel, in October 2013, when we welcomed presentations from Jacquelyn Campbell on 'Femicide and fatality from intimate partner violence', Naeemah Abrahams on 'Defining femicide in South Africa', and Rebecca and Russell Dobash on 'Female homicide victimization by men in the United Kingdom'. During the second meeting in Hafnarfjordur, Iceland, in September 2014, Janet P. Stamatel spoke on 'Building concepts and definitions regarding femicide', Capitolina Díaz on 'International definitions of femicide', and Michael Platzer lectured on the project 'Femicide: A global issue that demands action'. Furthermore, during the annual conferences in Lisbon in March 2014, Zaragoza in March 2015, Ljubljana in May 2016 and the final conference in Malta in March 2017, there were relevant presentations and discussions on definitions. It was clear that appropriately defining the term was critical to the work of the other COST Action working groups on prevention, data collection and culture, but first and foremost it was critical to all of us to enable us to conduct any research on the issue. So in Working Group 1 on definitions, the focus was on the following four questions:

1. What is femicide?
2. Does femicide include girls as well as women?
3. Does femicide include infanticide?
4. Is femicide the murder of women because they are women, or is femicide simply a non-gendered homicide (of any woman)?

Conceptualizing

Any word has a particular etymology. Some words bring forth a political purpose. This is the case here. In this section, we will discuss some achievements in identifying the most important definitions of femicide, deciding why these definitions are relevant and whether the different definitions imply different notions of femicide. The originator of the femicide concept is American feminist Diana H. Russell who, in 1976 at the first International Tribunal on Crimes against Women stated: "I chose the new term femicide to refer to the killing of females by males because they are female" (Russell, 2011). Though the word femicide was already known in the Anglo-Saxon world, Russell added critical political meaning to it and placed it within a broader feminist politics framework. Subsequently, Russell refined the concept as a 'misogynist killing of women by men' and an extreme manifestation of sexual violence – an addition suggested by Liz Kelly that highlights the gendered nature of forms of violence against women and focuses on the man's desire for power, dominance and control (Radford, 1992: 3–4). Kelly (1988) proposed that an essential element of the femicide concept is framing it as a form of sexual violence and an extreme form of violence in the continuum of sexual violence against women.

Very close, though not identical, is the concept of *feminicidio* developed by Mexican anthropologist and feminist Marcela Lagarde y de los Ríos and common in Latin America. Inspired by works of Russell and Radford (1992), Lagarde (2008) coined the term *feminicidio* in the early 1990s. It was translated from the English 'femicide' to describe and provide a theoretical framework for the dramatic rise in extreme violence against women and killings of women in Mexico, and particularly in Ciudad Juarez. She developed *feminicidio* in a more contextual way and added impunity as a critical element, that is, a failure of state authorities to prosecute and punish perpetrators. Nevertheless, Latin American legislations use both words interchangeably: feminicide and femicide (Grzyb and Hernandez, 2015). Such a conceptualization makes femicide/feminicide a state crime tolerated by public institutions and officials, a form of gender-based discrimination, and grounds for international accountability of states for human rights violations

(Corte Interamericana de Derechos Humanos, 2009).[1] For example, in Mexico, the General Law on Women's Access to a Life Free of Violence (2007) defines femicidal violence as 'the most extreme form of gender violence against women, produced by the violation of their human rights in public and private spheres and formed by a set of misogynist actions that can lead to the impunity of society and the State and culminate in the homicide and other forms of violent death of women' (article 21) (UNODC, 2014: 52).

It is noteworthy that the framing of violence against women as the obligation of a state to prevent the crime also prevails in Europe, as reaffirmed in the Istanbul Convention (2011). The Council of Europe Convention on preventing and combating violence against women and domestic violence is based on the understanding that *violence against women is a form of gender-based violence that is committed against women because they are women*. It is the obligation of the state to address it fully in all its forms and to take measures to prevent violence against women, protect its victims and prosecute the perpetrators. Failure to do so would make such violence the responsibility of the state. The convention leaves no doubt: there can be no real equality between women and men if women experience gender-based violence on a large scale and state agencies and institutions turn a blind eye.

The idea of femicide was introduced by the feminist movement in order to politicize and challenge male violence against women. From the very beginning it accounted for a range of specific forms of lethal violence against women, such as, for example, so-called honour killings and killings of prostitutes. With the passing of time, however, the definition

---

[1] The so-called Campo Algodonero case of Inter-American Court of Human Rights from 16 November 2009: Claudia Ivette González, Esmeralda Herrera Monreal y Laura Berenice Ramos Monárrez (Casos 12.496, 12.497 y 12.498) contra los Estados Unidos Mexicanos.

has become progressively diluted and confused, broadened by some authors to any killing of a women and thus divested of its political connotation (Alvazzi, 2011). This widening and depolitization of the concept occurred in part as a result of a growing research interest in violence against women, in order to facilitate comparative studies across countries. It was also, however, due to its political and legal recognition in many countries. Measuring femicide is extremely challenging due to a number of reasons (Bloom, 2008: 147). Even if the homicide is recorded in criminal records, often there is no information regarding possible motive, how it took place or the gender of the victim and/or perpetrator.

United Nations documents define femicide/feminicide as the gender-related killing of women that can take many forms (intimate partner femicide, killings of women due to accusations of sorcery/witchcraft, so-called honour killings, killings in the context of armed conflict, dowry-related killings, killings of aboriginal and indigenous women, killings as a result of sexual orientation or gender identity and so on), and recognize its scarce reporting and prosecuting by official authorities (UN General Assembly, 2012: 6–7; UNODC, 2014: 52). Finally, the Vienna Declaration on Femicide describes femicide as the killing of women and girls because of their gender, which can take the form of, inter alia:

- the murder of women as a result of domestic violence/ intimate partner violence;
- the torture and misogynist slaying of women;
- killing of women and girls in the name of so-called 'honour';
- targeted killing of women and girls in the context of armed conflict;
- dowry-related killings of women and girls;
- killing of women and girls because of their sexual orientation and gender identity;

- the killing of aboriginal and indigenous women and girls because of their gender;
- female infanticide and gender-based sex selection foeticide;
- genital mutilation related femicide;
- accusations of witchcraft;
- other femicides connected with gangs, organized crime, drug dealers, human trafficking and the proliferation of small arms. (Laurent et al, 2013: 4)

In 2017 the European Institute for Gender Equality (EIGE) put forward two definitions: a general one, which is drawn from the Vienna Declaration of the Academic Council on the United Nations System (ACUNS) stated above, and a statistical one that limits femicide to intimate partner femicide and deaths of women as a result of some harmful practices.[2] It seems thus that key elements of the notion of femicide are its gender dimension

---

[2]   Source: EIGE's (2017) Gender Equality Glossary definition of femicide:

> 'The term femicide means the killing of women and girls on account of their gender, perpetrated or tolerated by both private and public actors. It covers, inter alia, the murder of a woman as a result of intimate partner violence, the torture and misogynistic slaying of women, the killing of women and girls in the name of so-called honour and other harmful-practice-related killings, the targeted killing of women and girls in the context of armed conflict, and cases of femicide connected with gangs, organised crime, drug dealers and trafficking in women and girls.'

Developed definition of femicide for statistical purposes:

> 'The killing of a woman by an intimate partner and death of a woman as a result of practice that is harmful to women. Intimate partner is understood as former or current spouses or partners, whether or not the perpetrator shares or has shared the same residence with the victim.' (http://eige.europa.eu/rdc/thesaurus/terms/1128)

and the acknowledgement that it can take various forms across the world.

After reviewing texts and definitions of homicide, the following questions remained or were raised: (a) Is femicide to be considered an extreme form of violence against women? (b) Is femicide a gender-based killing? (c) Is femicide only a killing of women by men? (d) Is femicide to be considered only in cases of intentional killings of women? (e) Is femicide only when women are killed in the context of intimate partner violence? (f) Does the term femicide also include girls? (g) Can gender-based prenatal sex selection, also known as 'son preference', count as femicide? Despite their apparent banality and repeatability, these questions are important, because in order to be able to compare and analyse data on femicide, there must be clarity as to what is being counted. On the other hand, the questions can also be considered irrelevant, since women die regardless of the definition that is placed on the act. In the end, what is of utmost importance is that 'We want our counting to count for women!'

During the annual conference of the COST Action IS1206 held in March 2015 at the University of Zaragoza, we collected contributions from other working groups relevant to our work. Working Group 2 on reporting supported the definition of femicide as killings of females because they are female. From the perspective of data collection, however, the importance of beginning with a broader definition and separate categories was pointed out. They maintained that this would allow us to move forward to a deeper analysis, as the motives and details of the cases are often unknown, either in statistics or in other information systems. Thus, the following was suggested for pragmatic reasons. In the first step, all killings of women on national and international levels should be counted as possible cases of femicide. In the second step, specific categories of cases that are often counted, and where it is known that gender and gender relationships play a relevant role, should be extracted: for example, intimate partner killings (as one of the most common forms), killings in the context of sexual violence, sex-based abortions, so-called honour-related killings, hate crimes against LBTIQ people,[3] as well as against women and girls. In most countries it will be possible to count intimate partner violence at least as an extra category. In the third step, other cases of killings of women and girls should be further investigated in order to demonstrate whether or not gender might play a relevant role; here case studies on the basis of newspaper reporting, court and police information, and further qualitative studies could be helpful. This information should also be recorded in systematic databases to be built up within monitoring systems.

Working Group 3 on culture elaborated in a more nuanced way on the culture/gender and femicide link. The exchange within the group began by discussing the meaning of culture, and an agreement was reached that in this context it includes social norms, gender roles, and the ideas of femininity and masculinity. It then asked: 'How does murder come to happen in a specific culture?' While there was an understanding that 'culture' is sometimes used to legitimate murder and to justify honour killings, it was noted that care must be taken not to essentialize various communities. This means that we must go 'beyond culture'. This is especially important because often when culture is the topic, it may shift to the idea of 'migrant culture', or minority culture, although all communities, whether majority or minority, also have cultures (including social norms and gender roles) that need to be taken into account. Additionally, there must be an awareness of the discourse on multiculturalism, and the debate on migration, integration and rights, as it may impact on how femicide in the context of culture is explained. Most definitions of femicide include women killed by men or women, because they are women. It was noted that not only men kill women, but also mothers or aunts or grandmothers who reproduce the patriarchal system in which they have been

---

[3] Lesbian, bisexual, trans, intersex and queer.

immersed, and, as a result, there have been cases where women kill female babies or young girls. This means that restricting the definition of femicide to only women killed by men would not be appropriate. In conclusion, Working Group 3 argued that the definition of culture is multidimensional along different layers. In relation to femicide, one must look at the emic (insider) and etic (outsider) perspectives in intercultural situations and transnational contexts.

Working Group 4 on prevention stated that a complete definition of femicide in terms of its prevention would take into consideration different levels of prevention: primary, secondary, tertiary and quaternary. The real prevention of femicide has to be based on all of these levels, since carrying out an intervention only when there is clear risk, and the perceived posed threats are high, is insufficient. Prevention of femicide has to deepen its roots into a much broader framework, as it is acknowledged that even in most evolved and democratic countries, with well-intentioned policies, legislation and services, women are still killed as a consequence of male-dominated culture (whether overtly so or covertly). A clear agenda that addresses femicide, and more broadly, violence against women, has to address all parties at all four levels of prevention. The quaternary level of prevention, and therefore its definition, should also take into account the needs of victims after the apparent end of the risk. In this regard, there was an acceptance of Russell's (Radford and Russell, 1992) definition based on the opinion that femicide has culturally rooted origins in a masculinist and misogynist context.

Definitions and beyond

A clear and operational definition of femicide is important. But that in itself does not solve the problem. In policy-making terms, the target is to tackle and stop the violent deaths of women and girls everywhere. Since femicide is an extreme manifestation of violence against women, according to the authors of this chapter, all provisions of the Istanbul Convention regarding policy responses shall apply to combating femicide. The Istanbul Convention calls for integrated policies and data collection (chapter II). Furthermore, the Istanbul Convention requires that one or more official bodies (in every state) is designated or established to be responsible for the coordination of the collection of data, analysis and dissemination of its results. This data must include data on femicide.

The same body shall also to be responsible for the implementation, monitoring and evaluation of policies and measures to prevent and combat the various forms of violence against women and domestic violence. Once again, this must specifically include prevention of and combating femicide. Moreover, the convention obliges states to allocate appropriate financial and human resources for the adequate implementation of integrated policies, measures and programmes to prevent and combat all forms of violence against women and domestic violence, including those carried out by nongovernmental organizations and civil society. A coordinated approach helps in the collation of data. This is especially important since currently data on violence against women and domestic violence is not easily available at a national level in most European countries. Data on femicide is even more difficult to acquire, and therefore requires action to be taken by all countries that have ratified the convention to ensure that such data becomes available. Consensus on a clear and practical definition is fundamental in order to produce clear data, which is also necessary for the monitoring system to work. Furthermore, a clear and practical definition is also needed for awareness-raising, which is a piece of the puzzle that is necessary in order to create policies to prevent the violent death of women and girls everywhere.

Recommendations to policy makers can be provided at three levels: the European level (EU and Council of Europe), the national level (central or federal governments) and the local level (city councils and municipalities). Each of these authorities shape policies and coordinate institutions relevant in combating violence against women and gender equality enforcement. Recommendations may include:

- drafts of special legislations based on a clear and comprehensive femicide definition;
- sharing and implementing evidence-based best practices;
- improved methodologies for dealing with cases of femicide;
- practices for improved coordination among services;
- new services;
- provisions to impede impunities across borders.

Conclusions

A working definition of femicide should be the starting point for everything. Once we know how to define the 'problem', it should lead us and enable us to see a solution, within our context. In order to do so we need to build a system of data collection. Once we have the data it will be possible to show society and policy makers the magnitude of the problem (raise awareness), to convince them to tackle it on a policy level and to work towards prevention. A clear data collection and observation system is essential to raise awareness – to persuade, show and prove that femicide is a tangible problem that concerns all of us. It has to help us provide a clear picture of what is happening, to enable us to create and implement evidence-based policies and practice, and then to monitor and evaluate.

Foerster (2003) claims that even if we do not have an agreed specific definition of femicide, what remains important at the end of the day is how we deal with it. We need to reclaim Diane Russell's political definition of femicide: simply put, a woman is killed because of her gender. By claiming the word 'femicide' in its original political meaning, we make it possible to acknowledge that patriarchy, and the resultant gender inequality that pervasively continues to exist, are at the root of the problem. Juan Manuel Iranzo puts it like this:

> Feminicide: the killing of a woman because some man or men, although occasionally also some women who accept men's values, has or have sentenced her to death adducing whatever reasons, motives or causes, but nonetheless actually and ultimately because he or they believe she has defied (the words they often use are 'offended' or 'insulted') patriarchal order (in their words 'honourable' societies) beyond what her judge (often but not always the same person who kills her) is prepared to tolerate without retaliating in that way. (Iranzo, 2015: 1)

So it would appear that two 'forms' of definition are required, both intricately connected and necessary. At the base of our work and permeating throughout our work we need to maintain the clear political meaning of the word femicide – for without it we will go astray. But alongside it we need to agree what 'counting' data (quantitative and qualitative) is essential, for without it we cannot persuade, demonstrate and convince policy makers and legislators to create the services we require to prevent and combat this most extreme form of violence against women and girls.

References

Alvazzi del Frate, A. (2011) 'When the victim is a woman', in GD (Geneva Declaration) Secretariat, *Global burden of armed violence 2011: Lethal encounters*, Cambridge: Cambridge University Press, pp 113–44, www.genevadeclaration.org/fileadmin/docs/GBAV2/GBAV2011_CH4.pdf

Bloom, S. (2008) *Violence against women and girls: A compendium of monitoring and evaluation indicators*, Chapel Hill, NC: MEASURE Evaluation, http://cpwg.net/resources/violence-against-women-and-girls-bloom-2008/

Castoriadis, C. (1975) *The imaginary institution of society*, Cambridge, MA: MIT Press.

Corte Interamericana de Derechos Humanos (2009) *Caso González y otras ('campo algodonero') vs. México, sentencia de 16 de noviembre de 2009*, www.corteidh.or.cr/docs/casos/articulos/seriec_205_esp.pdf Foerster, von H. (1972) 'Responsibilities of competence', *Journal of Cybernetics*, 2(2): 1–6.

Foerster, von, H. (2003) *Understanding understanding: Essays on cybernetics and cognition*, New York: Springer.

Grzyb, M. and Hernandez, M. (2015) '"Still a long way ahead": criminalisation of femicide and addressing impunity in Latin America: recent developments', in M. Dimitrijevic, A. Filip and M. Platzer (eds) *Femicide: A blobal issue that demands action* (Vol. IV), Vienna: ACUNS, pp 84–93

Iranzo, J. M. (2015) 'Reflections on femicide and violence against women', Working paper on femicide (unpublished), GESES. Universidad de Zaragoza.

Kelly, L. (1988) *Surviving sexual violence*, Portland, OR: Polity Press.

Lagarde y de los Ríos, M. (2008) 'Antropologia, feminismo y politica: violencia feminicida y derechos humanos de las mujeres', in M. Bullen and C. Diez Mintegui (eds) *Retos teoricos y nuevas practicas*, Donostia: Ankulegi Antropologia Elkartea, pp 214–18.

Laurent, C., Platzer, M. and Idomir, M. (2013) '"Femicide": the power of a name', in *Femicide: A global issue that demands action*, Vienna: ACUNS, p 4.

Radford, J. (1992) 'Introduction' in J. Radford and D.E.H. Russell (eds) *Femicide: The politcs of woman killing*, New York: Twayne, pp 3–12.

Russell, D.E.H. (2011) 'The origin and importance of the term femicide', www.dianarussell.com/origin_of_femicide.html

United Nations General Assembly (2012) *Report of the Special Rapporteur on Violence against Women, Its Causes and Consequences, Rashida Manjoo*, A/HRC/20/16.

United Nations Office on Drugs and Crime (UNODC) (2014) *Global study on homicide*, Vienna: UNODC, www.unodc.org/documents/gsh/pdfs/2014_GLOBAL_HOMICIDE_BOOK_web.pdf

THREE

Data collection: challenges and opportunities

Monika Schröttle and Ksenia Meshkova

Introduction

This chapter documents the main result of the work of Working Group 2 on data collection and reporting. The central aims of the group were: (1) to identify differences and similarities in data collection on femicide at national and international levels across Europe, and (2) to develop recommendations for European countries and organizations on how to improve their femicide data collection.

Comparison of country-specific data

The working group started with concrete comparisons of country-specific data on femicide and compared methodologies of data collection as well as femicide rates. Furthermore, comparisons on related topics, such as non-lethal forms of violence against women, the Gender Equality Index, homicide rates in general and the socioeconomic situation in European countries, were conducted in order to find patterns and relevant correlations.

We found that data collection systems were typically based on national criminal statistics. They were usually not comparable between countries. Even though most states record the sex of the victim and/or offender in the homicide data, the definitions of homicide and the categories that are included in data collection, as well as the modes of data collection, are not identical. Moreover, not all states include the sex of victims *and* offenders for a specific case of homicide in the dataset. Furthermore, in many countries the data recorded fails to include the motives of the crimes as well as the relationships between victims and offenders (for example, whether the crime was committed against an intimate partner).

Comparison of country maps

Another interesting task of the working group was to compare country maps indicating the extent of femicide with country maps on other related topics. For example, it could not be confirmed that the extent of violence against women in general, the extent of homicides in general, the state of gender equality in the country and the duration of active policies on violence against women have a direct correlation with the extent of femicides.

Figures 3.1 and 3.2 show that countries with high rates of violence against women reported in the European Union Agency for Fundamental Rights (FRA) survey are not per se countries with high femicide rates.

Figure 3.1: Femicide rates across Europe based on the WHO Mortality Database 2014

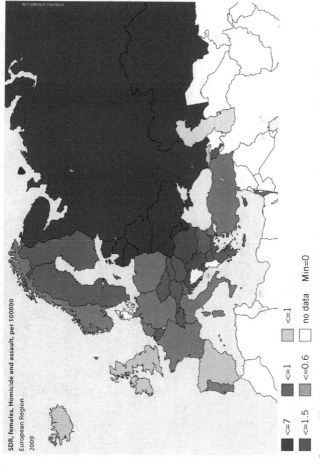

SDR, females, Homicide and assault, per 100000

European Region

2009

<=7   <=1

<=1.5   <=0.6   no data   Min=0

<=1

Source: Map based on the World Health Organization Mortality Database (WHO, 2014)

Figure 3.2: Physical intimate partner violence against women across Europe

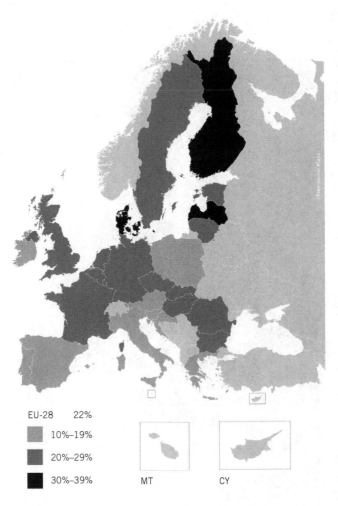

Physical and/or sexual partner violence since the age of 15, EU-28 (%)

Source: FRA gender-based violence against women survey dataset, 2012

Furthermore, in countries with a high Gender Equality Index score (such as Sweden and Finland), femicide rates are not low (cf. Figures 3.1 and 3.3).

Figure 3.3: Gender Equality Index scores of European countries

The scale is based on the range in scores (max-min) divided by 4.

Source: Gender Equality Index, EIGE, 2017

Though some countries with high homicide rates (such as Lithuania, Estonia and Latvia) also show high femicide rates, we could not prove a clear relationship between femicide rates and general homicide rates (cf. Figures 3.1 and 3.4). National statistics show a decrease in homicides in European countries over the past decades, while the rates of femicides tend to stay stable.

Figure 3.4: Homicide rates per 100,000 population by country

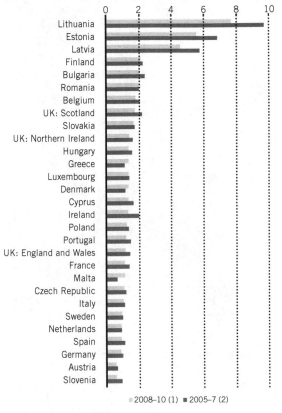

■ 2008–10 (1) ■ 2005–7 (2)

(1) Netherlands, 2009–10
(2) Estonia and Latvia, 2006–7; Ireland, 2007 only

Source: Eurostat, 2013

Furthermore, a country's poverty rate is not clearly connected to the rate of femicides (cf. Figures 3.1 and 3.5).

Corradi and Stöckl (2016) produced a map on the start of government action on violence against women, showing European states who started governmental action in this area in the 1970s, 1980s and 1990s. Though this map does not provide information on the impact or continuity of state activities, it is remarkable that early state actions and long-lasting activities have not substantially contributed to lower femicide rates (cf. Figures 3.1 and 3.6).

Figure 3.5a: At-risk-of-poverty rate by sex, total, 2013

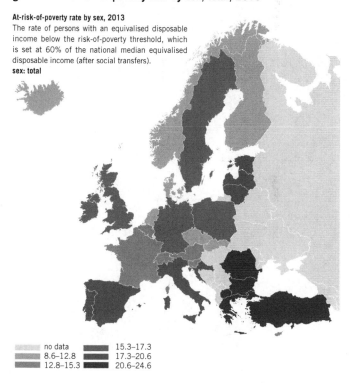

Source: Eurostat, 2013

Figure 3.5b: At-risk-of-poverty rate by sex, females, 2013

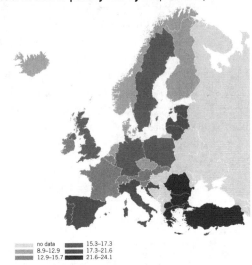

Source: Eurostat, 2013

Figure 3.5c: At-risk-of-poverty rate by sex, males, 2013

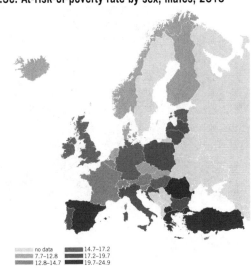

Source: Eurostat, 2013

Figure 3.6: State action on violence against women

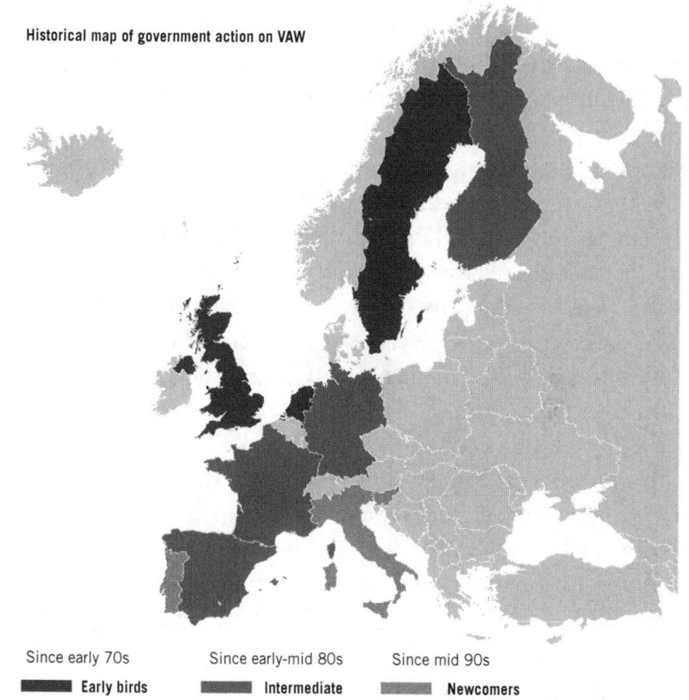

Historical map of government action on VAW

Since early 70s	Since early-mid 80s	Since mid 90s
Early birds	Intermediate	Newcomers

Source: Corradi and Stöckl, 2016

It was not possible to conduct secondary analysis with various data sets in the working group. Nevertheless, the comparison shows that connections between different factors and their influence on the extent of femicide seem to be more complex than anticipated and have to be investigated further on a European level.

Information on European databases and observatories

Within Working Group 2 of the COST Action IS1206 on 'Femicide across Europe', a further step was taken to collect information on several European databases and observatories related to femicide. Collected information included descriptions of the organizations and good practice for femicide data collection. It was found that some countries already have databases on femicide: for example, Italy (Piacenti et al, 2013, Piacenti, 2015), the UK (Smith, 2016; Women's Aid/Nia, 2017), Spain (Feminicidio.net, 2016) and Serbia (Women against Violence Network, 2015). Furthermore, international bodies are intending or have already started collecting information that is focused primarily on or includes data on femicides, for example, Eurostat, the European Homicide Monitor (EHM), the European Women's Lobby, EIGE and the United Nations Office on Drugs and Crime (UNODC) Femicide Watch (cf. Chapter 6 in this book).

Institutions that had developed or started to develop databases on femicide were invited for a common meeting by the COST Action in Brussels in 2015, and have since started to build a coalition for the future coordination of the work, with a view to establishing a European Observatory on Femicide (EOF).

Concept mapping study

Within the working group, a concept mapping study was conducted with the goal of assembling expert opinions on what strategies are needed and feasible in order to promote, develop and implement an integrated femicide data collection system across European countries (Vives-Cases et al, 2016). The study followed concept mapping methodology, and involved 28 members of the COST Action on femicide from 16 countries, who generated strategies of femicide prevention and then rated them according to relevance and feasibility. The result of the study was a conceptual map, which consisted of 69 strategies structured in 10 clusters, belonging to two main domains: 'political action' and 'technical steps'. Participants of the study identified promotion of media involvement as the most feasible strategy. Strategies to raise public awareness and institutionalize national databases were considered the most relevant.

Identifying relevant data and indicators for prevention

In the last year of the COST Action, in 2016–17, the working group on data collection and the working group on prevention came together in order to determine what types of data and information are important and needed for the prevention of femicides. It became clear that the crime statistics alone on the prevalence of femicides in countries are not sufficient. Further information must be collected in order to understand the reasons and background behind femicides, and to identify possibilities to intervene and to prevent killings. Therefore, it also has to be determined whether victims and offenders were already known to several institutions, and if there was a possibility to intervene earlier and save the victim. Moreover, it is necessary to collect more comparative data (comparison across time and between countries/regions) in order to identify where political institutions and societies were successful in preventing femicides.

Femicide data collection in Europe today: challenges and critique

The study of femicide statistics from various European countries showed that data collection in Europe presents a high heterogeneity. Police and crime statistics still remain the most important official national source of data. In most of the countries where systematic criminological data collection on homicide exists, homicides or murders of women are included and can be disaggregated by gender, though the definitions of the acts differ because they are related to different criminal codes. In some countries female homicides by intimate partners can be identified, as well as information on the victim–perpetrator relationship, but in general these statistics do not allow further differentiation of other types of femicide in non-partner relationships (cf. Eurostat, 2016 and Chapter 6 in this book); information on (gendered) motives of the cases of homicides is in general not available. In some countries the disaggregated data has not yet been made public or is inaccessible and has to be obtained by special request, usually through the police and justice systems or general crime statistic systems.

The data is structured in various ways that make comparisons across countries challenging. Central problems of data collection are related to differences in definitions, missing data and missing information on the background motives of the cases as well as the victim–perpetrator relationship.

In most countries femicide is not defined as a distinct type of crime. The understanding of femicide also differs from country to country; in some countries the term is not used or does not exist. Even if the definitions were harmonized, it would still be difficult to collect data on femicide because in the current data there is no information on the reasons or motives for the killing of women. Current types of data collection do not make it possible to answer the question of whether a woman was killed because she is a woman or not.

For several national and international bodies that collect data on femicide, the second most important source of information is the media. Here, more information can be gained on backgrounds, motives, victim–offender relationships and whether people were known to institutions prior to the murders. It seems to be practical to combine both data from crime statistics and information from the media to deepen the knowledge of the cases and gain information relevant for prevention. A very small number of countries can additionally use death statistics from the health sector, though the investigation showed that this data may not be compatible with the more accurate and aggregated data from crime statistics.

A further source of information on femicides could be support systems (shelters and counselling centres). However, it still has to be ascertained if and how their knowledge on cases could be included in the development of elaborate databases at national and international levels.

Recommendations for data collection

Improved knowledge base on patterns/developments

It is very clear that Europe needs more accurate data and statistics on femicide in order to gain a better understanding of the issue of femicide as well as data and information that are necessary for prevention.[1] The aim is to collect meaningful data, and to evaluate and document it in a way that is useful for social policies and practice.

Though accurate data comparison will not be possible in the near future, it should at least be possible to compare:

- **Background/risk factors**
  To answer the questions:
  - What are the relevant influencing and risk factors (for example, gender inequalities and dependencies, economic situation/deprivation, prior domestic violence, availability of weapons, alcohol abuse and so on)?
  - Are there similar/different risk factors in countries/regions?

- **Estimates of prevalence of femicide** (related to inhabitants/related to all homicides)
  To answer the question:
  - How prevalent is femicide?

---

[1] As Marceline Naudi, member of Working Group 2 and Malta's Management Committee member in COST Action IS1206, 'Femicide across Europe', said in a meeting with stakeholders in Brussels in November 2015: "We want counting to count for women!"

- **Development over time**
  To answer the question:
  - Is femicide decreasing/increasing/staying stable?
  - And to further investigate reasons for different developments.

- **State reactions/law/convictions**
  To answer the questions:
  - How does the state react (over time)?
  - How does this contribute to prevention or persistence of the problem?

Improved definition and data collection strategy

The working group suggests following a common strategy for data collection across Europe in order to successively overcome the problems of incomparability and different definitions.

First, all data on intentional homicides with female victims should be collected, as this is the central basis for cases of femicide. Then, further information on victims and perpetrators and their relationship should be collected. Intimate partner homicides against women should be documented and clearly defined as femicides due to their gendered character. The same should be done for the killing of women in the context of sexual violence and prostitution. For other forms/contexts, investigation of the cases in greater detail is necessary (including background, motives and possible reasons of the killings of women).

As it is often impossible to get detailed information on the (gendered) motives of the cases, it is important to collect further qualitative information and to conduct case studies or analyse cases for a fuller understanding of the contexts and causes of the problem.

Several national and international databases have already been established or are being planned. It is important to harmonize their strategies in order to gain valid and comparable data and information. The European Observatory on Femicide that has been established in Malta could be the institution to collate and pool these strategies and to lead European countries to a common strategy for data collection on femicide.

Multiple sources for data collection

Central sources from which to obtain quantitative and qualitative data on femicide are:

- international data reports and data collection systems (for example, those of Eurostat and UNODC, the Geneva Convention on Small Arms, the Sophia Institute, the European Homicide Monitor and EIGE);
- published and unpublished national criminological data and sociological studies on femicide in each country;
- press information from the police and the media (the press information has to be seen as a relevant source to get further background information on the cases – certainly, the results have to be rechecked and verified by the police and the justice systems in order to obtain valid data).

Data and information on femicide has to be collected on all regional, national and international levels by several institutions (police, courts, support services and health systems). It is recommended that national databases are established to systematically collect, evaluate and publish national data on femicide, and to harmonize the definitions as well as the procedures of data collection as far as is possible. The national data will build the basis for regularly available European and international data on femicide to be collected within the European Observatory on Femicide. This data should at least allow disaggregation by sex of victims and perpetrators, the victim–perpetrator relationship (at a minimum: intimate partner and non-partner femicide), prior history of domestic violence and previous institutional interventions. It should furthermore include detailed information on the definitions and the procedure of data collection. It is also important to train those in charge of data collection as well as journalists and practitioners reporting on the issue.

Possible and minimum indicators

Working Group 2 of the COST Action on femicide has defined minimum indicators and further relevant indicators that have to be collected, investigated and further developed by the international research community and other institutions responsible for or active in data collection.

Minimum indicators

- **Basic data on victims and perpetrators:**
  - This should include number of cases, victims, perpetrators, genders of both victims and perpetrators per case.
  - It is important to provide continuity of data collection and comparability in time (and between countries/ regions) to monitor the (development of the) problem.

- **Context of the murder:**
  - Here the victim–perpetrator relationship (at least intimate partner homicides by current/former partners against women) should be identified.
  - If available, some basic information on the nature and motives of the cases should be provided.

Further indicators

- Further demographic information on victims and perpetrators (indications for possible risk factors)
- Information on prior domestic violence, protection orders and services used (whether the case was known to institutions/intervention and protection measures put in place/support provided)
- Convictions (response of the state system)

With this basic set of information, the most important data for understanding the issue of femicide and improving prevention would be available. Detailed descriptions of the cases would make it possible to check if and how intervention and prevention would have been possible.

International cooperation in data collection

For international collection of data on femicide, existing institutions should collaborate in a coalition in order to avoid doubling activities. Some actions and institutions, such as EIGE, the European Homicide Monitor, the Group of Experts on Action against Violence against Women and Domestic Violence (GREVIO), WAVE and the UNODC Femicide Watch, have already begun to collect data at the international level. They could and should include the experiences of already existing national data collection systems, for example, those in Italy, Spain, the UK and Germany. The European Observatory on Femicide (EOF) could be very successful within a coalition or cooperation of existing data collection systems and activities. It should furthermore be integrated into national/international data collection systems on violence against women, especially with regard to monitoring of the Istanbul Convention (GREVIO, EIGE, Eurostat).

Conclusions

The discussions in Working Group 2 of the COST Action have shown how to monitor the issue of femicide in the future and with what types of data and information. We have seen that it is reasonable to create scientifically based monitoring with a proper strategy together with all national and international partners. On the one hand, such a structure must promote the creation of comparable national databases. On the other hand, it must systematically involve existing international systems of data collection and their experience.

It became very clear during discussions that the collection of police data alone would not be sufficient for analysing the cases in the detail needed for prevention and intervention. Therefore, many countries have chosen the strategy of collecting information on all the cases known to the media and collating it with the criminological data and – insofar as is possible – data recorded by the health and support systems. This strategy makes it possible to obtain more background information on femicides, which is important for future prevention and early interventions.

In order to stabilize the collection of data and information at the European level, it is important to publicly finance work resources at the national level in order to create and continuously update national databases in a way that makes international comparison possible. Furthermore, a scientifically based monitoring body must coordinate data collection and supply it to joint databases. Only in this way will it be possible, in the long-term, to create a bigger pool of data that allows deeper analysis and prevention of the problem at the European level.

References

Corradi, C. and Stöckl, H. (2016) 'The lessons of history: the role of the nation states and the EU in fighting violence against women in 10 European countries', *Current Sociology*, 64(4): 671–88.

EIGE (2017) 'Gender Equality Index', http://eige.europa.eu/gender-equality-index/2015/countries-comparison/index/map

Eurostat (2013) 'At-risk-of-poverty rate by sex 2013', http://ec.europa.eu/eurostat/tgm/mapToolClosed.do?tab=map&init=1&plugin=1&language=en&pcode=tessi010&toolbox=legend

Eurostat (2016) 'Intentional homicide victims by age and sex - number and rate for the relevant sex and age groups [crim_hom_vage]', http://appsso.eurostat.ec.europa.eu/nui/show.do?dataset=crim_hom_vage&lang=en

Eurostat Statistics Explained (2013) 'Homicide rate per 100 000 population, average per year, 2005–2007 and 2008–2010', http://ec.europa.eu/eurostat/statistics-explained/index.php/File:Homicide_rate_per_100_000_population,_average_per_year,_2005-2007_and_2008-2010.png

Feminicidio.net (2016) 'Geofeminizido', www.geofeminicidio.com/geoinf.aspx?idPais=70

FRA (2014) *Violence against women: An EU-wide survey: Main results*, http://fra.europa.eu/sites/default/files/fra-2014-vaw-survey-main-results-apr14_en.pdf

Piacenti, F. (2015), 'EURES: Characteristics and dynamics of femicide in Italy', Unpublished presentation, COST meeting, Rome, 16 January 2016.

Piacenti, F., Fusaro, N., Valido, M., Vassura, V., Coccia, F. and Cesarini, I. (2013) 'L'omicidio volontario in Italia. Rapporto EURES 2013. In collaborazione con l'Agenzia ANSA', www.spaziosociale.it/public/allegati/3172013114259-Omicidio%20volontario%20in%20Italia.pdf

Smith, K. I. (2016) 'Counting dead women', https://kareningalasmith.com/counting-dead-women/2015-2/

Vives-Cases, C., Goicolea, I., Hernández, A., Sanz-Barbero, B., Gill, A. K., Baldry, A. C., Schröttle M. and Stöckl H. (2016) 'Expert opinions on improving femicide data collection across Europe: a concept mapping study', *PLOS ONE*, 11(4): e0154060, https://doi.org/10.1371/journal.pone.0148364

WHO (2014) European Mortality Database, http://data.euro.who. int/hfamdb

Women against Violence Network (eds) (2015) *Femicide: Murder of women in Serbia: Quantitative – narrative report 2014*, www. zeneprotivnasilja.net/images/pdf/FEMICIDE_Narrative_and_ Quantity_Annual_Report_for_2014.pdf

Women's Aid/Nia (2017) *Femicide census: Profiles of women killed by men: Redefining an isolated incident*, https://1q7dqy2unor827bqjls0c4rn-wpengine.netdna-ssl.com/wp-content/uploads/2017/01/The-Femicide-Census-Jan-2017.pdf

FOUR

Understanding and preventing femicide using a cultural and ecological approach

Christiana Kouta, Santiago Boira, Anita Nudelman and Aisha K. Gill

Introduction

Femicide – the killing of a woman or girl, in particular by a man (often an intimate partner), on account of her gender – is not only a complex phenomenon but also a leading cause of premature death among women globally (Corradi et al, 2016; Vives-Cases et al, 2016). To effectively manage or prevent cases of femicide – and other forms of violence against women – it is therefore necessary to comprehend the sociocultural and ecological parameters that may influence it (Vives-Cases et al, 2016). While viewing femicide from a cultural perspective increases its complexity, it is nevertheless essential to consider not only how Western and non-Western cultures influence myriad individual, organizational, communal and societal attitudes regarding male violence against women, but also how these attitudes can in turn determine public policies and the state's actions in relation to such violence (Flood and Pease, 2009; Gill et al, 2016; Vives-Cases et al, 2016). In taking such a cultural and ecological perspective, this chapter seeks to explore and understand femicide in European countries.

While the literature suggests that many approaches can be used to understand and prevent violence against women (Gill, 2018), the effectiveness of the ecological model, which emerged in the late 1970s (Bronfenbrenner, 1979), has been emphasized in particular. The ecological model posits a multifaceted approach that was initially applied to the study of child abuse in the social field. It has since been applied to explaining other forms of violence, particularly domestic violence. On the premise that no single factor can explain violent behaviour, the World Health Organization (WHO), for example, also adopts a multicausal perspective in its approach to explaining violence (WHO, 2002). The ecological perspective offers not only a useful working methodology for achieving a broader vision of a problem that we want to understand (Vives-Cases et al, 2016) but can also be applied to promote educational initiatives, interprofessional collaborations and community- and population-based efforts to prevent and decrease violence (WHO, 2012).

Certain cultural and social norms may support different types of violence. For example, traditional beliefs that men have a right to control or discipline women make women vulnerable to violence by intimate partners (WHO, 2009). Given that femicide can be viewed as a sociocultural phenomenon, the ecological model becomes a 'socioecological' lens through which to effectively analyse many social problems, including femicide and violence against women (Centers for Disease Control and Prevention, 2002). Thus, this perspective facilitates understanding of the numerous sociocultural factors that either put people at risk of violence or protect them from experiencing or perpetrating violence, as understanding these factors is important in terms of determining risk of femicide. According to Boira et al (2017), a relationship exists between the different factors of the ecological model's subsystems regarding understanding intimate partner violence, and they argue that this interrelationship increases the risk of femicide. The model also indicates that social elements such as patriarchal values or the role of the family may increase that risk (for example, in a rural setting as a consequence of social control, in traditional family environments or when the action of the state is fragile) (Vives-Cases et al, 2016). Similarly, it is important to note the closeness of the relationship between culture and symbolic violence, and how this form of symbolic violence is present in the daily environment in which femicide and violence against women occur across many cultures (Thapar-Björkert et al, 2016).

Sociocultural approaches highlight the influence of social norms, values and cultural beliefs that are widespread in a given society (Corradi et al, 2016) and which are essential to researching femicide because analysing sociocultural factors related to intimate partner violence and femicide – and how these manifest in culturally diverse settings (Kouta et al, 2017) – is integral to understanding and preventing femicide. Cultural differences affect all spheres of society and, specifically, the ways in which gender relations are structured in terms of power relations and the different manifestations of gender violence (Gill et al, 2016). To develop a better understanding of the prominent role that culture plays in gender violence, it is essential to address the complexity of a contemporary global Europe.

Thus, in order to develop a better understanding of the prominent role that culture plays in gender violence, this chapter addresses the relationship between culture and femicide in the context of a contemporary global Europe – a conglomeration of native and foreign cultures formed by various migratory movements throughout history – and, drawing on the relevant literature, determines appropriate ways to respond to and prevent femicide (Gill et al, 2016).

Defining femicide from a cultural perspective

Our working definition of femicide includes the killing of females by males merely because they are females. In this way, we adopt both the proposal in the Vienna Declaration on Femicide (Laurent et al, 2013) and all the definitional aspects discussed in Chapter 2. On that basis, the current chapter proposes that the different forms of femicide encompass – but are not limited to – intimate partner-related killings (Vives-Cases et al., 2016), honour crimes, dowry-related murders, forced suicide, female infanticide, gender-based sex-selective foeticide, and the targeted killing of women during wars and in the context of organized crime. Understanding femicide from a cultural perspective thus involves considering the specific nature of femicide crimes, for example, analysing murders of women which have been committed in the name of 'honour' by their partners, former partners or family members, as in such cases the murder can be a consequence of adultery, homosexuality, divorce, attempted sexual assault or refusal to marry (Gill, 2018). Addressing these crimes from the perspective of culture not only involves encountering potential differences between European countries and the cultural specificities of the peoples who inhabit them, but obliges us to confront the hegemonic culture, where the 'expert's' voice (that is, social actors that generate accepted social discourses – politicians; religious, economic and cultural leaders; journalists; and in some cases researchers) is often placed alongside subordinate and much less visible aspects of culture which are manifested in practices, norms, beliefs and so on. In this sense, a cultural dialogue can radically affect how we define and explain the causes of femicide, in that it makes us broaden our perspective on and understanding of the many factors at play that can lead to femicide (Shalhoub-Kevorkian and Daher-Nashif, 2013).

Further, adopting a broader definition of femicide implicates circumstances that perpetuate misogynous attitudes and/or socially discriminatory practices against women (Gill, 2018), because this broader definition encompasses, for example, cases of death caused by or associated with gender-based selective malnutrition or trafficking women as prostitutes and drug mules (Gill et al, 2016). As it is often difficult to decide whether women and girls have been killed because of their gender, researchers investigating femicide generally include all killings of females in the first stage of analysis and then differentiate between cases that are more or less influenced by gendered contexts and motives (WHO, 2012; Balica and Stöckl, 2016; Vives-Cases et al, 2016).

Why use a cultural perspective?

Attempts have been made to explain femicide using different positions, paradigms and theoretical perspectives; of these, the ecological model and the multicausal approach proposed by Corradi et al (2016) are suitable, as they accommodate the incorporation of cultural elements into explanations of the complex phenomenon of femicide.

As Kouta et al (2017) indicate, in various European countries, cultural factors contribute to instances of femicide. It is therefore crucial to analyse how each country addresses aspects such as, for example, masculinity and femininity, gender equality, domestic violence and femicide laws, patriarchal ideology, traditional values, the role of religion in society, culturally specific forms of femicide, and media coverage of femicide and violence against women. Although patriarchy remains dominant in European societies, each European country has its own specific context in which the factors identified above interact. These differences should be taken into account in order both to explain and to prevent incidences of violence against women, including femicide, because it is impossible to understand femicide without considering the particular cultural environment in which it occurs. This cultural approach must also acknowledge the manifestations of a country's local and foreign cultures, and how they relate to one another. The interactions of differing beliefs, attitudes and behaviours may be positive or negative and may represent either protective or risk factors for femicide. For example, as Nudelman et al (2017) note, in the case of migrant women suffering gender-based violence in Europe, the interaction between different cultural realities can prove crucial in terms of exacerbating these women's risk of femicide. Nudelman et al's (2017) research also explores several important factors that contribute to this risk in terms of the host state's attitude towards migrant women, any language or legal barriers in the host country, pressure from the women's local community in the host country and the women's access to support resources. Weil (2016), too, reports incidents where migrant women were forced to marry or were abducted by their husbands and suffered severe domestic violence in both their native and host countries, in her research on 'failed femicides'. Male control over women's lives, bodies and sexuality is strengthened by 'culturalization', because, as Shalhoub-Kevorkian and Daher-Nashif note, it is males who act within a patriarchal structure, who plan, implement and turn a blind eye to women's needs, who silence abuse, who fail to address women's calls for help and who are able to stop the killing (Shalhoub-Kevorkian and Daher-Nashif, 2013: 18).

Studies such as those by Sanz-Barbero et al (2014) and Balica and Stöckl (2016), which address the situation of migrant women who suffer gender-based violence in European countries, highlight the forms, causes and contexts of gender violence. Others explore not merely the legal, economic and sociocultural barriers these women face (see, for example, Martínez-Roman et al, 2017), but also how the violence affects them in terms of their quality of life, societal exclusion and health (Fernbrant et al, 2014). Globally, the gender-related killing of women and girls is associated with structural discrimination, that is, discrimination related to gender, culture and class (Kouta et al, 2017). Furthermore, in Western societies, structural discrimination not only persists, but is glorified in certain cultures, such as in misogynistic and racist contexts.

Broadly, the literature indicates that femicide is often influenced by sociocultural dynamics and practices and that cultural practices can exercise a strong influence within a community or country. According to Weil and Mitra vom Berg (2016), cultural and social practices such as marriage at an early age and arranged and dowry marriages may lead to femicide. The killing of women in relation to dowries or to 'save the family honour' is a tragic occurrence and an explicit illustration of embedded, culturally accepted discrimination against women and girls (Gill, 2018), as the act of murder may sometimes be encouraged by other family members (WHO, 2012). In addition, it seems that what can be seen as a 'culture of femicide' encourages abortions of female babies in Indian society.

Adopting the ecological approach allows us to extend our consideration of femicide beyond the individual circumstances of the victims and perpetrators. It also enables us to identify how the biological, social, cultural and economic factors in each case can either reduce or increase a woman's risk of violence and death (Boira et al, 2017), because it exposes the complex interplay between individual, relationship, community and sociocultural elements (Heise, 1998). For Fulu and Miedema (2015), the ecological model highlights the ways in which global movements leave their mark on the social structures, relationships and experiences of men and women. Providing an understanding of the multidimensional causes of violence can thus enable us to more effectively respond to and prevent different forms of violence against women.

It is important to note that certain cultural factors exacerbate the risk of femicide occurring. Taking that into account, Corradi et al (2016) propose a multicausal model based on three levels of explanation, each of which identifies the empirical variables associated with femicide. The first level includes variables related to individuals' psychological organization, psychosocial habits and interactions at the micro level. The second (meso) level examines the networks and subsystems of the relationships through which the couple, the extended family and the other actors involved are linked. Finally, the third (macro) level incorporates complexity science and sociocybernetics analyses (Castellani and Hafferty, 2009) 'along two axes, from a linear–Cartesian to a systemic approach, and from a static to a dynamic model' (Corradi et al, 2016: 13). These ecological, systems and multicausal perspectives may be of significant help in understanding the phenomenon of femicide (Freysteinsdóttir, 2017).

Nevertheless, studies show that gender–based violence and femicide are not usually discussed or analysed from an ecological or socioecological perspective (Corradi et al, 2016). This oversight often leads to a lack of cultural and gender sensitivity when addressing such acts of violence among the general population across Europe, and even more so when addressing acts of violence against women from cultural minorities and migrants in specific European contexts. This lack of sensitivity also creates additional barriers to identifying potential victims and developing meaningful ways of relating to minority/migrant women, their families and their communities. Moreover, sociocultural misunderstandings and/or insensitivity when addressing gender–based violence hinder appropriate care and prevention, and may even result in femicide.

To understand the specific sociocultural and ecological context in which femicide takes place, it is important to focus both on local and minority cultures within Europe and the interactions between them. In the case of migrant women in Europe who are victims of ongoing gender–based violence, for instance, the interaction between their different cultural realities may lead to an increased risk of femicide caused by myriad factors that also act as barriers to their seeking assistance (Nudelman et al, 2017). By helping to formulate effective, culturally appropriate and preventative measures in response to femicide, the ecological approach can further our understanding of and responses to these issues.

Effectively responding to and preventing femicide

The ecological approach focuses on the interplay between individuals, their personal relationships (including those with their families) and their communities, as well as with wider bodies, such as services, institutions and legislation (Bronfenbrenner, 1979; Boira et al, 2017). This approach can identify how the influence of country-specific biological, sociocultural and economic factors can either reduce or increase the risk of violence and death (Boira et al, 2017). Thus, when implementing public policies, drawing on an ecological approach would allow for a more integrated analysis that could accurately identify femicide risk factors, and these could then be incorporated into policies and strategic action programmes (Kouta et al, 2017).

Given that the term femicide is not widely known and is often misunderstood or confused with homicide (simply the killing of one human by another without reference to the victim's gender), femicide often goes unreported as a very particular type of murder. However, recommendations based on both ecological and multicausal approaches may enable policy makers and professionals in relevant fields to better comprehend the issue and respond in meaningful and effective ways (Laurent et al, 2013). A thorough understanding of femicide in specific sociocultural contexts should be promoted to enhance culturally sensitive awareness, care and prevention, which may in turn enable potential victims to overcome barriers to seeking assistance and support. To achieve this end, it is essential to work simultaneously across all relevant levels of society and to involve professionals such as healthcare providers and educators, members of the judiciary and police, authorities and other functionaries dealing with gender violence, as well as communities and women at risk (Gill et al, 2016).

All relevant service providers dealing with gender violence across Europe should receive intensive training that imparts cultural/social knowledge of various groups in the population, as well as culturally and gender-sensitive ways to address these groups and gain their trust. In terms of victims of violence who are migrants, minorities and/or of different ethnicities, service providers must be aware of and consider the cultural and symbolic norms, beliefs and perceptions embedded in these victims' countries of origin, including the accepted types of social relationships within these cultures, since lack of knowledge and cultural sensitivity may influence victims' accessing services.

Although healthcare providers could play a crucial professional role in raising awareness of and preventing femicide, especially when dealing with minority groups and migrants, they often fail to discover or correctly identify the underlying causes of violence among women who access healthcare services; thus, they are not able to offer culturally meaningful care (Leskošek et al, 2015). To rectify this situation, they should be sensitized through appropriate training to enhance their knowledge and comprehension of the cultural traditions, beliefs, perceptions and practices regarding family and gender relations among the different population groups they serve. This training will strengthen their ability both to understand situations that occur in specific sociocultural contexts and to offer more meaningful support to victims of violence. In particular, they should develop a trust-based relationship with women who are victims of violence, including survivors of attempted femicide and/or their relatives. The knowledge and skills gained through such training will enable them to explore each woman's particular history of violence and threats against her, since specific types of threats that are made may be related to societal norms in the male aggressor's country of origin. It is therefore critical that healthcare providers be trained to ask specific questions in a sensitive way to identify some of these warning signs at an early stage and thus prevent femicide from occurring (Gill et al, 2016; Nudelman et al, 2017).

Healthcare professionals should also be aware of the potential sources of support available to women and those to which they can refer women, in the case of formal/official support systems. These include the woman's personal support network, such as her family, friends and workmates, as well as formal/ official systems of support. Women's use of the latter depends on their familiarity with these systems and perception of their effectiveness. Barriers to access arise if a woman feels that these systems pose a threat to her either because she fears stigma and discrimination or, for example, if she is member of an ethnic minority or is in the country illegally.

Legal professionals also play a critical part in dealing with gender-based violence and femicide. Unfortunately, these acts often elicit an inadequate response from the legal system, especially in the area of criminal justice. If lawyers and court officers are to comprehensively address gender-based violence and femicide, they should undergo sensitivity training. This training could lead to a stricter application of existing laws and better consideration of female gender-based violence victims in court hearings, since lack of respect for such victims generally poses a barrier to women filing complaints and seeking justice. In the case of migrants and cultural minorities, using professional mediators and interpreters from the relevant cultural community for translation and support should be encouraged. Further, since gender violence is deeply rooted in both cultural norms and gender roles, the legal system and its representatives need to be aware of such structural causes and to account for them when debating cases and making decisions and reaching verdicts (see Gill et al, 2016).

The police are also at the forefront when it comes to handling femicide and violence against women, as they are often the first people to talk to female victims of gender-based violence and attempted femicide. For this reason, police officers should also undergo sensitivity training to ensure that they address these women in a culturally and gender-sensitive way, that they are adequately prepared to offer support and protect such women, and that they can encourage women to report acts of violence that may occur against them in the future (see Gill et al, 2016). Handling these issues more sensitively and more skilfully will enable police not only to collect more detailed data about incidents involving violence against or killings of women, but also to identify elements such as sociocultural factors related to religious and minority groups or migrants, and situational and risk factors that might have contributed to the reported incident. Gathering data related to femicide is fundamental, since it can assist victims by better equipping the police to identify risk factors or warning signs and make femicide more visible, and also by increasing awareness among policy makers and professionals as well as community members more broadly.

All relevant professionals and service providers should find ways to make information about gender-based violence and femicide accessible and meaningful for women from various cultural backgrounds, should develop proactive responses and should minimize any bureaucracy that could hinder the taking of urgent action. In addition, essential culturally and gender-sensitive information should be made available in various languages and formats.

Following the different levels proposed in the ecological model, awareness of femicide must also be enhanced among political policy makers at local and national levels, since they are in a prime position to address the issue and prompt change that may lead to meaningful reforms. Such change could include promoting gender equality by implementing policies that make it possible for women to leave abusive partners, for example, protection (in shelters or safe houses), financial support (child support and access to free healthcare) and rehabilitation, while acknowledging and providing for these women's sociocultural backgrounds (see Gill et al, 2016: 1–4).

Finally, the media – printed, visual and electronic – is a major source of awareness-raising about social issues such as gender violence and femicide. At present, the latter is often regarded as a minor issue that occurs only among minority groups and thus does not present a threat to the wider society. As this attitude may lead to underreporting or sensational commentaries that increase fear and gender stereotyping, it is vital to improve journalists' understanding of femicide and to facilitate their access to reliable sources when reporting an incident of it (Dart Center for Journalism and Trauma, 2014). In addition, femicide should be called by its name in the media, rather than by misleading terms such as 'love crime', 'crime of passion' or 'jealousy crime', in order to further promote public knowledge and awareness of the circumstances under which femicide can arise (Gill et al, 2016: 1–4).

Conclusions

The cultural perspective mediates the way in which people and institutions interpret and act in response to reality. Thus, having an understanding of culture is fundamental when it comes to facilitating understanding of the relationship between femicide and social issues such as the construction of masculinity and patriarchy, the role of the family and honour, human trafficking or migration and refugee policies. Understanding femicide using a cultural and ecological approach can develop in-depth awareness of, and responses to, gender-based violence and femicide. In fact, as Michau et al (2015) note, adopting this approach appears to be crucial in terms of prevention, as the socioecological model considers the different levels (individual, interpersonal, community and societal) involved in the causes of femicide.

Responses to femicide must take place across all these levels, that is, with individuals and victims' families; with communities, including schools and places of worship; with local and official institutions; and among relevant professionals and policy makers. Interventions should be specifically designed for different sociocultural groups and contexts, taking into account additional determinants (financial, political, environmental, occupational and migration-related) that may affect gender violence, and should consider how the multicausal effect operates in relation to femicide.

Further, culturally appropriate prevention and intervention approaches must entail community engagement education, especially in relation to intimate partner violence and the associated risk of femicide. Research and surveillance regarding killings of women remains sparse, and legislation, where it exists, is often poorly enforced and easily circumvented. Advocacy to change laws that permit these types of crimes is thus essential (WHO, 2012; Vives-Cases et al, 2016). Raising awareness of these crimes among stakeholders and policy makers by collecting and analysing available data, including court cases and other key sources of information, is especially valuable for protecting women's rights and preventing femicide. Greater awareness of and sensitivity to femicide and its causes is necessary to enact appropriate culturally and gender-sensitive and preventative measures. For minority and migrant women in Europe in particular, understanding and identifying the relationship between cultural context and risk of femicide is vital if we are to circumvent those risks and stop acts of violence before they occur.

References

Balica, E. and Stöckl, H. (2016) 'Homicide–suicides in Romania and the role of migration', *European Journal of Criminology*, 13(4): 517–34.

Boira, S., Tomas-Aragones, L. and Rivera, N. (2017) 'Intimate partner violence and femicide in Ecuador', *Qualitative Sociology Review*, 13(3): 30–47.

Bronfenbrenner, V. (1979) *The ecology of human development: Experiments by nature and design*, Cambridge, MA: Harvard University Press.

Castellani, B. and Hafferty, F. (2009) *Sociology and complexity science: A new field of inquiry*, Berlin: Springer.

Centers for Disease Control and Prevention (2002) 'The social-ecological model: A framework for violence prevention', https://www.cdc.gov/violenceprevention/pdf/sem_framewrk-a.pdf

Corradi, C., Marcuello-Servos, C., Weil, S. and Boira, S. (2016) 'Theories of femicide and their significance for social research', *Current Sociology*, 64(7): 975–95.

Dart Center for Journalism and Trauma (2014) 'Covering homicide: a tip sheet for college media advisors, editors and student journalists', http://dartcenter.org/content/covering-homicide

Fernbrant, C., Emmelin, M., Essén, B., Östergren, P. and Cantor-Graae, E. (2014) 'Intimate partner violence and poor mental health among Thai women residing in Sweden', *Global Health Action*, 7(1): doi: 10.3402/gha.v7.24991.

Flood, M. and Pease, B. (2009) 'Factors influencing attitudes to violence against women', *Trauma Violence Abuse*, 10(2): 125–42.

Freysteinsdóttir, F. J. (2017) 'The different dynamics of femicide in a small Nordic welfare society?' *Qualitative Sociology Review*, 13(3): 14–29.

Fulu, E. and Miedema, S. (2015) 'Violence against women: globalizing the integrated ecological model', *Violence against Women*, 21(12): 1431–55, https://www.ncbi.nlm.nih.gov/pmc/articles/PMC4638316

Gill, A. K. (2018) 'Eliminating violence against women and girls: the case for an effective international law', in R. Manjoo and J. Jones (eds) *The normative gaps in the legal protection of women from violence: Pushing the frontiers of international law*, London: Routledge, 1–9.

Gill, A.K., Kouta, C. and Nudelman, A. (2016) 'Briefing paper on the role of service providers, criminal justice staff, policy makers and journalists in addressing femicide', Prepared for COST Action IS1206.

Heise, L. (1998) 'Violence against women: an integrated, ecological framework', *Violence Against Women*, 4(3): 262–90, https://www.ncbi.nlm.nih.gov/pubmed/12296014

Kouta, C., Rousou, E., Freysteinsdóttir, F, Boira, S. and Naudi, M. (2017) 'Gender and socio-cultural perspectives through femicide case studies', *Journal of Community Medicine and Health Care*, 2(2): 1013.

Laurent, C., Platzer, M. and Idomir, M. (2013) *Femicide: A global issue that demands action*, Vienna: ACUNS.

Leskošek, V., Lučovnik, M., Pavše, L., Sršen, T. P., Krajnc, M., Verdenik, I. and Velikonja, V. G. (2017) 'The role of health services in encouraging disclosure of violence against women', *Slovenian Journal of Public Health*, 56(4): 220–26, https://www.ncbi.nlm.nih.gov/pubmed/29062396

Martinez-Roman, M., Vives-Cases, C. and Pérez-Belda, C. (2017) 'Immigrant women suffering from IPV in Spain: The perspectives of experienced social workers' *Affilia – Journal of Women and Social Work*, 32(2): 202–16.

Michau, L., Horn, J., Bank, A., Dutt, M. and Zimmerman, C. (2015) 'Prevention of violence against women and girls: lessons from practice', *Lancet*, 385: 1672–84.

Nudelman, A., Boira, S., Tsomaia, T., Balica, E. and Tabagua, S. (2017) 'Hearing their voices: exploring femicide among migrants and culture minorities', *Qualitative Sociology Review*, 10(3): 49–68.

Sanz-Barbero, B., Rey, L. and Otero-García, L. (2014) 'Health status and intimate partner violence' [Estado de salud y violencia contra la mujer en la pareja], *Gaceta Sanitaria*, 28(2): 102–8.

Shalhoub-Kevorkian, N. and Daher-Nashif, S. (2013) 'Femicide and colonization: between the politics of exclusion and the culture of control', *Violence against Women*, 19(3): 295–315.

Thapar-Björkert, S., Samelius, L. and Sanghera, G. (2016) 'Exploring symbolic violence in the everyday: misrecognition, condescension, consent and complicity', *Feminist Review*, 112(1): 144–62.

Vives-Cases C., Goicolea, I., Hernández, A., Sanz-Barbero, B., Gill, A. K., Baldry, A. C., Schröttle, M. and Stöckl, H. (2016) 'Expert opinions on improving femicide data collection across Europe: a concept mapping study', *PLOS ONE*, 11(4): e0154060, https://doi.org/10.1371/journal.pone.0148364

Weil, S. (2016) 'Failed femicides among migrant survivors' *Qualitative Sociology Review* 12(4): 6–21, www.qualitativesociologyreview.org/ENG/Volume39/QSR_12_4_Weil.pdf

Weil, S. and Mitra vom Berg, N. (2016) 'Femicide of girls in contemporary India', *Ex Aequo*, 34: 31–43, http://exaequo.apem-estudos.org/artigo/femicide-of-girls-in-contemporary-india

WHO (2002) 'World report on violence and health: summary', Geneva: World Health Organization, http://www.who.int/violence_injury_prevention/violence/world_report/en/summary_en.pdf

WHO (2009) 'Violence prevention – the evidence. Changing cultural and social norms that support violence', Geneva: World Health Organization, http://www.who.int/violence_injury_prevention/violence/norms.pdf

WHO (2012) 'Understanding and addressing violence against women. Femicide', Geneva: World Health Organization, http://apps.who.int/iris/bitstream/10665/77421/1/WHO_RHR_12.38_eng.pdf

FIVE

Prevention of femicide

Anna Costanza Baldry and Maria José Magalhães

Introduction

When referring to 'prevention of femicide', we refer to actions at the individual, family, and social and community levels that can reduce the likelihood of women being killed because of their gender. Strategies for prevention of femicide differ depending on the definition of femicide and the cases to which we refer. For example, prevention of femicide in intimate partner relationships is different from prevention of the killing of trafficked women, or girls being subjugated and killed. These distinct femicides are set in different contexts, involve different risk factors and therefore require different prevention strategies. However, what all femicides share is a single motivation: femicide, according to the feminist approach, and the one that enables us to explain its prevalence worldwide, is the killing of women because they are women, regardless of whether it is perpetrated by the victim's partner, ex-partner or a non-partner. The killing of women constitutes an extreme exercise of power against them; it is perpetrated to establish control (Radford and Russell, 1992).

This masculine, misogynist perspective on gender also increases the perception that violence is an acceptable way of managing disputes, conflicts and problems. Within femicides, it is possible to identify recurrent patterns: namely, homicide occurring as an ultimate means to degrade, silence and subjugate women.

Femicide prevention efforts require both research and intervention. They include combating a culture based on relationships in which men have dominance over women, and not only those actions immediately preceding the killing. In fact, prevention can be set at different levels, depending on the level of risk factor it focuses on. Causes of femicide are multilevel: employing an ecological approach, risk factors can be identified at the individual, interpersonal and community levels. Back in 1998, Heise described how the ecological framework is the most exhaustive to explain violence against women, as it looks not only at which risk factors are relevant but at how they interact in a dynamic way. As Heise explains, 'besides serving as a framework for research, an ecological approach provides a way to better understand differences among abusers' (Heise, 1988: 284). Risk factors at the *individual level* may be related to the perpetrator's personality, abuse of alcohol and/ or drugs, childhood abuse, a history of violence, or masculine honour-based beliefs (Baldry and Pagliaro, 2014). At the *interpersonal level*, factors include, among others, the type and status of the relationship between victim and perpetrator, and family influences. At the *community level*, risk factors include the surrounding culture and its predominant beliefs about violence, previous prevention campaigns and legal definitions.

Prevention of femicide is therefore a complex issue, as ideally all these levels should be addressed. In this chapter, we will focus on some aspects of prevention of femicide in order to highlight a number of avenues for possible action, including femicide fatality reviews, and risk assessment to identify relevant and critical risk and vulnerability factors. In addition, we will address primary prevention as an essential step for challenging patriarchal culture, and developing research, activism and intervention (Fitz-Gibbon and Walklate, 2016).

Femicide fatality reviews

Fatality reviews in cases of femicide are a process whereby a homicide is analysed with the aim of identifying all potential factors that might explain its occurrence and locating any possible failure in the system. The intention is not to hold anyone other than the perpetrator responsible but, rather, to offer recommendations for improving procedures, communication, decision-making processes and so on, based on what was done or omitted that might have led to failure to prevent the perpetrator killing his victim (Richards, 2003; Fitz-Gibbon and Walklate, 2016; Sharp-Jeffs and Kelly, 2016; Dawson, 2017).

Practitioners, with the help of researchers, first developed domestic fatality review teams approximately twenty years ago, as a new way to enhance understanding of the complex processes leading to homicide in intimate partner relationship. Fatality reviews in the US and Canada were created to address homicides with a special focus on intimate partner femicide (IPF) also in order to understand what could have been done to prevent the killing and to develop intervention or prevention strategies (see, for example, Watt, 2008). The outcomes of these reviews are directed towards policy recommendations, promotion of training, increasing awareness and modification of existing procedures. In 2011 and 2014, the UK also set up domestic homicide reviews (DHR), which addressed homicides within the family context (see Durfee et al, 2002; Rimsza et al, 2002; Webster et al, 2003; Dawson, 2017).

In order for fatality review teams to fulfil their remit, they need to be authorized by the legislature or established under executive orders to ensure they have the power to act with confidentiality, accountability and immunity (see also Dale et al, 2017). Specific legislations are needed to allow the fatality teams to gain access to confidential information related to possible witnesses or family members, and to interview them in order to review the homicide and gather as much information as possible looking at the circumstances and characteristics around the death. Legislations and related executive orders are also formulated to allow leeway for local discretion regarding the convening agency and the membership of the team (Websdale et al, 2001).

Not all teams and all reviews follow the same procedure (cf. Dawson, 2017). Members of the fatality review team meet on a regular basis to review cases of IPF and develop recommendations for changes to policies and practices on the basis of their findings (Websdale, 1999; Websdale et al, 2001; Watt, 2008; Sharp-Jeffs and Kelly, 2016). The team can consist of as many representatives as possible from different sectors and institutions that might have played a role in the lives of both victim and perpetrator. It is up to the team members to decide whom to hear from and what type of research to undertake. The fatality review team may also share information they come across with relevant agencies, in addition to providing recommendations to them (Websdale, 1999; Websdale et al, 2001; Dawson, 2017).

The main aim of most fatality review teams is to prevent future fatalities through instigating changes at the system level, thereby involving different actors (Websdale, 1999). As Watt explains:

These review teams model values, honesty and accountability and seek to identify breakdowns or gaps in service delivery, focusing less on individual accountability and more on system-wide coordination (Websdale et al, 1999). As opposed to placing blame on agencies for IPF (Intimate Partner Homicide), any errors committed in the risk assessment, in the procedure adopted before the killing... are viewed as inevitable aspects of coordinated delivery of complex services and perpetrators are ultimately held responsible for the deaths of their victims. (Watt, 2008: 57–9)

Addressing each single femicide case, looking at what happened; identifying the possible characteristics of the case at the individual, interpersonal, and social and community levels; and adopting an ecological approach can be of use to prevent other instances of femicide.

Each team reviews its case by adopting different methods, depending on the availability of resources, the commitment of different agencies, the experience of members and the number of femicides to analyse. Some teams, such as those examining cases of IPF, review any killings perpetrated by a current or former (female or male) intimate partner. Other teams review all deaths that occurred in the context of domestic violence (including suicides of perpetrators, as well as homicides of children, new intimate partners, intervening parties or responding law enforcement officers) (Dawson, 2017). Teams are organized in such a manner that they either review closed cases – in which the perpetrator has already been convicted – or open cases – where the case is still pending (Websdale, 1999; Websdale et al, 2001). The former method is much more common because law enforcement and the judicial system do not always favour sharing information that might compromise a conviction (Watt, 2008), although this varies from country to country. The information amassed by domestic violence fatality review teams is collected via several sources of information, including police records, coroners' files, autopsy reports, court documents, medical records, mental health records, social service reports, newspaper accounts and victim services records. In some cases, family members, friends or professionals are also interviewed (Watt, 2008; Dawson, 2017).

An advantage of fatality reviews in cases of femicide is that at the end of the review the team prepares a report indicating the method adopted, the sources of information used and the outcome of the review. It also provides recommendations for the improvement of service delivery, and these are also published online (see, for example, Dawson, 2017). The femicide review might also be tasked with implementing and evaluating changes to service delivery and assessing their efficacy in their respective agencies, based on the recommendations they put forward, though the review will not always follow up on the implementation of these changes (Websdale, 2003; Watt, 2008; Sharp-Jeffs and Kelly, 2016;).

It is important to note that the conclusions of fatality reviews are often grounded in examinations of several cases, rather than a single case. This enables the team to address best management strategies, based on different levels of risk. Such reviews also have the advantage of linking together all possible risk factors preceding the femicide, exploring the risk factors related to the perpetrator, the vulnerability factors of the victims, and any contextual and interpersonal variables and circumstances.

Results from reviews on intimate partner femicide cases, one of the most frequent forms of femicide in Western countries, have demonstrated some emergent recurrent patterns that may be classified according to different risk factors and positioned at different levels, related to the perpetrator, the victim and the community. For this reason, when referring to prevention of femicide, another important aspect to take into consideration is risk assessment.

Risk assessment

Femicide risk assessment is a procedure targeted at prevention (Hart, 2008). It is based on the principle that some femicide cases can be prevented because some of these murders are preceded by an escalation of violence, threats and other lethal risk factors. Risk assessment allows us to identify the presence of risk and vulnerability factors, and to establish their nature and relevance to the violence. An assessment of the dynamic interaction of these risk factors renders it possible to improve understanding of the level of potential risk; this then opens up the choice of options for the most effective management strategies. By adopting an ecological approach (Heise, 1998), the different level of risk are addressed: individual, interpersonal, and social and community.

Risk assessment can be carried out using actuarial methods, whereby a list of risk factors is added together and the total is compared with a specific threshold number, above which the risk is considered to be high. These approaches are useful because the methodology allows for an 'objective' reference level, upon which decisions will be based (Campbell et al, 2003).

Other approaches, such as the professional structures procedures – for example, SARA (the Spousal Assault Risk Assessment) (Kropp and Hart, 2000; Baldry and Winkel 2008) – are based on the analysis of presence or absence of risk factors. These risk factors have been identified by reviewing cases and empirical practice as highly correlated to recidivism of violence, escalation of violence and even killing. Risk factors for recidivism of intimate partner violence are very similar to the risk factors for femicide. What Campbell and colleagues (2003) found in their study is that only a very few indicators can be considered as specific indicators of lethal violence. These are named as follows: attempted strangulation, threats with firearms, extreme severe violence and, most importantly, what the woman herself perceives as risk. Women, however, might underestimate the risk involved; in such cases, they may not be able to self-assess their own risk. Nonetheless, when a victim states that she 'fears he will kill her' (or her children or any other relative or friend), it is important to take these statements seriously.

Table 5.1: Risk factors for intimate partner femicide and recidivism of intimate partner violence (IPV)

Category	Risk factor
Perpetrator	
	Substance use problems[a]
	Criminal history[a]
	Previous IPV[a]
	Possession of firearms[a]
	Victim of child abuse/exposure to IPV[a]
	Mental health problems[a]
	Socially disadvantaged[a]
Victim	
	Socially disadvantaged and/or isolated[a]
	Previous IPV (same or other partner)[a]
	Mental health problems[a]
	Substance use[a]
Victim–perpetrator relationship	
	Relationship status (separated or still cohabiting)[b]
	IPV (same or previous relationship)[b]
	Stalking[b]
	Children from another relationship[b]
Community	
	Insufficient social support network[c]
	Insufficient community resources[c]
	Lack of coordination between community resources[c]
	Attitudes accepting of violence against women[c]
	Lenient legislations[c]
Lethality violence-related risk factors	
	Attempted strangulation *Threat to kill with a firearm* *Extreme fear of being killed on the part of the victim*

Source: Adapted from Dawson (2017) and Watt (2008).
Note: In italics, some 'specific' lethality risk factors.
Based on an ecological framework, risk factors in the table above are categorised as follows: [a] individual, [b] interpersonal, [c] community and social levels.

Primary prevention to challenge patriarchal culture

Following the overview on fatality reviews and risk assessment, this section focuses on other forms of prevention aimed at bringing about cultural and structural changes. As stated above, the prevention of femicide is a complex issue which may be approached in several ways. Literature on prevention, especially in the area of health studies, points to a holistic approach to prevention as an effective means of eradicating a problem. Some perspectives equate prevention with early intervention, that is to say, getting to the root of a problem before the problem emerges, and eliminating the conditions that facilitate its occurrence.

Until recently, authors identified three levels of prevention: primary – to prevent the problem before it occurs; secondary – targeting the problem at the early signs; and tertiary – targeting populations where the problem is located (Wolfe and Jaffe, 1999). Learning from other areas, such as health and crime prevention, authors have since extended the paradigm of prevention to two additional levels. Initially, there is a level of primordial prevention – creating a culture and life habits where the probability of occurrence of the problem would be residual; at the other end of the continuum is quaternary prevention – that is, the follow-up to tertiary prevention, which aims to assert the sustainability of the possible quality of life (Starfield et al, 2008).

Although there are diverse perspectives on femicide, several approaches focus on the pervasive patriarchal culture as the material and cultural basis for this crime. This view understands femicide as an extreme form of violence against women on the continuum of violence (Kelly, 1987, 1988), and violence against women as the utmost form of women's oppression in society (Hagemann-White, 1998). Taking femicide as a lethal form of patriarchal control over women's lives, the task of preventing femicide 'has certain parallels with the task undertaken by feminists working around violence against women in the 1970s' (Radford, 1992: 7). From this perspective, male violence is explained as a form of male dominance based on an imbalance of power in relationships featured in patriarchal society (Radford, 1992).

Naming the problem may be considered as the first step towards primary and primordial prevention. As part of 'women's right to name our experience' (Radford, 1992: 3), the understanding of the problem in its social, political and cultural context (Meneghel et al, 2013) – that is, extending the atomic/incidental perspective that only stresses the individual behaviour and the incident – is crucial to social and cultural change in relation to femicide. Data on the incidence of femicide accounts for a prevailing culture where women are still considered, to some extent, to be 'expendable'. Feminist analyses of violence against women centre on the structure of relationships in terms of a male-dominated culture, power and gender. Feminist explanations of violence against women consider gendered social arrangements and power as central (Taylor and Jasinski, 2011: 342).

Although femicide in intimate partner relationships is the more prevalent form, there are other forms of femicidal violence constituting part of that societal culture where the lives of women appear to be of minor importance.

Femicide takes many different forms, for example:

- racist femicide (black women killed by white men);
- homophobic femicide, or lesbicide, (lesbians killed by heterosexual men);
- marital femicide (women killed by their husbands or ex-husbands);
- serial femicide;
- mass femicide (including the deliberate transmission of the HIV virus by rapists);
- situations where women are permitted to die as the result of misogynous attitudes or social practices (female genital mutilation, illegal botched abortion);

- female infanticide;
- unnecessary lethal surgery (hysterectomies and clitoridectomies).

A comprehensive understanding will permit the creation of social and cultural conditions with the capacity to shift the patriarchal paradigm. Some acts of killing of women, such as those against lesbian women, black women and prostitutes, are still deemed to be of lesser gravity under the provisions of various legal reforms on violence against women.

The ultimate goal of femicide prevention is the eradication of this crime. In addition to fatality reviews and risk assessment as secondary and tertiary prevention, it is necessary to address the pertaining social and cultural factors within a comprehensive approach to prevention. As Nation et al (2003) attest, comprehensive prevention includes providing an array of interventions to address the salient precursors of the target problem, and extending these to primordial and primary prevention. For comprehensive strategies, there are two dimensions to consider – multiple interventions in multiple settings addressing the problem behaviour (Nation et al, 2003).

It is imperative that any comprehensive approach to primary prevention highlights femicide as a heinous crime, regardless of the social, cultural, ethnic or sexual status of the victim. Feminist literature has pointed out that femicide is a cruel reality, beyond the killing of women in the context of intimate partners or ex- partners, including the murder of women in contexts of sexual violence by known or unknown perpetrators, as in the case of the Ciudad Juarez murders in Mexico (Toledo Vásquez, 2008). Homophobia and racism demand to be addressed in order to develop the concept of women as persons of value in their own right. Recognition of heteronormativity as an oppressive dimension of patriarchal society can also facilitate the understanding of specific forms of femicide, namely, homophobic femicide and lesbicide. At the same time, 'an awareness of the complexities of racism, of the historical legacies of colonialism and imperialism, of the trap of appropriating black women's experiences to advance the political agendas of white feminism' (Radford, 1992: 8) forms part of a holistic programme to eradicate femicide (and violence against women). Racism is sometimes evident: visible either as exaggeration of the problem – perpetuating the stereotype of black men as more prone to violence than white men – or minimization of its importance – suggesting that violence is more acceptable in these communities. Authors such as Marcela Lagarde y de Los Ríos (2008, 2011) have stressed the avoidable nature of this hate crime, as an outcome of state neglect towards the human rights of women. Stressing the neglect of the state, Lagarde calls this crime *feminicidio*, a term that has been adopted within the penal codes of Mexico, Nicaragua, the Dominican Republic and Brazil.

This is an important point, in the sense that preventing femicide begins with effective action by the statutory agencies charged with the protection of women's lives.

Naming the problem and building a legal framework can contribute to increasing public awareness, and to diminishing tolerance of violence against women and femicide. Public awareness is best enhanced when people are able to identify the discernible dimensions and root causes of the problem.

Many femicides or attempted femicides are chronicles of deaths foretold (García Marquez, 1981); hence, it is possible to identify a number of dimensions at the foundation of these fatalities. As Caputi and Russell (1979: 426) assert, 'ironically, the patriarchy's ideal domestic arrangement (heterosexual coupling) is the most potentially femicidal situation'. Misogyny and sexism not only motivate gender violence (lethal and nonlethal), but distort the interpretation of the crime, as is visible in media coverage and other cultural expressions – for instance, in films (femicidal violence being the main theme of slasher films[1]), music, video games and so on.

Cultural factors of femicide are deeply embedded in society, cutting across class, ethnicity, religion or region of the globe. Male sexual proprietariness (Wilson and Daly, 1998) and a male sense that they are entitled to get what they want from women (Caputi and Russell, 1979) are among issues that should be targeted in prevention – challenging the cultural basis of femicide.

However, naming the problem, legal frameworks and public awareness raising are not sufficient to create the desired change. A comprehensive strategy to eradicate femicide also needs to focus on addressing gender inequality and improving the status of women.

Research has provided contradictory evidence concerning the comparison between the status of women and men and rates of femicide. Some authors have found higher female homicide rates where the status of women is more equal to that of men, while others have found that gender income inequality does not correlate with overall femicide rates (Taylor and Jasinski, 2011). Others still have shown that the educational status of women is not directly linked with prediction of femicide: some evidence shows that femicide increases when the woman's educational status is higher, whereas other research studies present data that indicates that the risk of femicide increases where the woman's educational status is lower (Taylor and Jasinski, 2011). Some authors have also brought evidence to the effect that the erosion of white male privilege can have lethal outcomes. Hence, in some countries, the advance of the status of women has actually been concomitant with an increase in lethal violence.

---

[1] 'Slasher': a subgenre of horror film, typically involving a psychopathic killer stalking and murdering victims in a graphically violent manner, often with a bladed tool, such as a knife, machete, axe, scythe or chainsaw.

Taking these data into consideration, some perspectives might argue against a prevention strategy based on challenging patriarchal society and culture. Without disregarding these research studies, however, there must be an acknowledgement, when considering a society's culture within a wider, historical context, that the changes in women's social status are only of recent origin. Furthermore, the increase in the status of some women is not synonymous with the eradication of the prevailing social representations of women and women's bodies: it does not mean that the social construction of the sexual objectification of women has undergone change. These individual changes do not challenge male sexual proprietariness (Wilson and Daly, 1998), the sense of male property ownership of women and children, and the hegemonic sense of entitlement to use force and violence to maintain control of women's lives (Campbell, 1992; Campbell et al, 2007). Nor are some individual social positions sufficient in themselves to balance the sexual contract (Pateman, 1988) of patriarchal, capitalist, heterosexist and racist society.

Hegemonic masculinity and emphasized femininity are still reproduced today by various agencies, social actors and institutional settings. Some young men learn to objectify women sexually through socialization with their peers, as well as other ways of learning masculinity, such as watching pornography, engaging in gang activity or other violent practices. Male fraternity and some male cultures include practices and/or discourses that support the abuse of women. Recent research also shows the emergence of rape culture and pro-abuse male peer support groups in cyberspace (DeKeseredy, 2011).

Challenging the social reproduction of women's oppression and/or subalternization calls for primary prevention, entering deeply into the cultural basis as well as challenging the symbolic violence against women (Bourdieu, 1989; Magalhães and Lima-Cruz, 2014). Educational studies have shown that the processes of cultural change are slow, requiring long, holistic and systematic interventions.

Romantic love (Gius and Lalli, 2014), jealousy, passion (Correa, 1981) and male sexual proprietariness (Wilson and Daly, 1998) represent a number of the social constructions of the heritage of modernity as elements at the foundation of the sexual contract in patriarchal society (Pateman, 1988). These dimensions of the 'private' and 'intimate' sphere, as opposed to the 'power' and 'public' domain, are inbuilt to the social dichotomies developed through modernity. The ultimate goal of primary and primordial prevention of femicide is to denaturalize and deconstruct the 'normalization' of violence against women in all its forms, including femicide.

Developing research, activism and intervention

Besides fatality reviews, risk assessment, and primary and primordial prevention, it is crucial to develop research and activism as well as appropriate intervention strategies and measures to address the issue of femicide across all the pertinent contexts.

The essential goal of research in general is to provide an understanding of and tools to decrease incidence of a social problem. Despite decades of relative 'invisibility' (Radford and Russell, 1992), research on femicide has expanded in recent years (Carcedo and Sagot, 2000; Glass, 2004; Carcedo, 2010; Fregoso and Bejarano, 2010; Lagarde, 2010; Romeva, 2013; Meneghel and Portella, 2017). However, in order to generate in-depth understanding, further research is required. This needs not only to be of a quantitative nature, but to incorporate a more holistic perspective. Some authors also stress the crucial relevance of disaggregating data accordingly, that is, in relation to ethnicity, 'race', marital status and age. Significantly, qualitative, in-depth research would have the potential to illuminate the complex, interwoven processes between human lives, as well as structural power relations and patterns of social change; this would allow opinion makers and policy makers to extend the vision of the problem to its sociostructural factors (Grana, 2001). Logically, this should also pave the way for improved legislation, social policies and educational programmes. While the victims of femicide cannot be heard, we are still able to listen to the victims of attempted femicides and study the impact of this crime on family, children, relatives and wider society. Research can also trace the changes in media portraits of femicide (Magalhães-Dias and Lobo, 2016), allowing policy recommendations on news production.

To date, we still lack a clear understanding of the connections between gender inequality and lethal violence against women. Hence, further research into the relationship between this form of violence and the changes in gender relations over time is essential in order to plan more effective femicide prevention.

Research also informs feminist activism (Rosa and Magalhães, 2016) and intervention.[2] One outstanding example is the naming of the Brazilian Law 11.340/2006 to prevent and combat violence against women as the 'Maria da Penha Law', in tribute to the surviving victim of an attempted murder – a woman who is fortunately still alive and fighting for the recognition of this crime as a violation of human rights.

Conclusions

This chapter has suggested six main areas for the prevention of femicide:

1. The establishment of a state obligation to ensure the human rights of women (Toledo Vásquez, 2008), including the

---

[2] For example, the authors of this chapter collaborated with the following groups and programmes, to whom they are indebted: the Combahee River Collective in Boston (a black feminist lesbian organization, 1974–80), the Repeal Attacks' and 'Murders of Women' groups in Britain, as well as symbolic initiatives.

enactment of appropriate legal measures to combat the murder of women in all situations, regardless of the women's social, economic, ethnic, marital or sexual status;

2. The acknowledgement of the gendered nature of this hate crime;
3. The treatment of femicide as a severe violation of human rights;
4. The development of more efficient and effective fatality reviews and risk assessments;
5. The creation of holistic, comprehensive and systematic educational programmes challenging patriarchal culture and contributing to a woman-friendly culture;
6. The development of quantitative and qualitative research to develop a better understanding of the problem.

These six preventive strategies do not cover all contingencies, insofar as femicide is embedded in the social construction of societal divisions between private and public life, and those between women and men. Nevertheless, taken together, they have the potential to make an impact and a valuable contribution to a progressive decrease in this horrific crime.

References

Baldry, A. C. and Pagliaro, S. (2014) 'Helping victims of intimate partner violence: the influence of group norms among lay people and the police', *Psychology of Violence*, 4(3): 334–47.

Baldry, A. C. and Winkel, F. (eds) (2008) *Intimate partner violence, prevention and intervention,* Hauppauge, NY: Nova Science.

Bourdieu, P. (1989) *O poder simbólico [Symbolic power]*, Rio de Janeiro: Bertrand.

Campbell, J. C. (1992) '"If I can't have you, no one can": power and control in homicide of female partners', in J. Radford and D. Russell (eds) (1992) *Femicide: The politics of woman killing*, New York: Twaine Publishers, pp 99–113.

Campbell, J. C, Webster, D., Koziol-McLain, J., et al (2003) 'Risk factors for femicide in abusive relationships: results from a multisite case control study', *American Journal of Public Health*, 93(7): 1089–97.

Campbell, J. C., Glass, N., Sharps, P. W., Laughon, K. and Bloom, T. (2007) 'Intimate partner homicide: review and implications of research and policy', *Trauma, Violence and Abuse*, 8: 246–69.

Caputi, J. and Russell, D.E.H. (1979) 'Femicide: speaking the unspeakable', *Journal of Personality and Social Psychology*, Sep–Oct: 424–30.

Carcedo, A. (2010) *No olvidamos ni aceptamos. Femicidio em Centro América, 2000–2006*, San Jose: CEFEMINA.

Carcedo, A. and Sagot, M. (2000) *Femicidio en Costa Rica: 1990–1999*, Costa Rica: Instituto Nacional de Mujeres (Colección Teórica no. 1).

Correa, M. (1981) *Os crimes da paixão [Crimes of passion]*, São Paulo: Brasiliense.

Dale, M., Celaya, A. and Mayer, S. J. (2017) 'Ethical conundrums in the establishment and operation of domestic/family violence fatality reviews', in M. Dawson (ed), *Domestic homicides and death reviews: An international perspective,* Guelph: Palgrave Macmillan, pp 229–56.

Dawson, M. (2017) *Domestic homicides and death reviews: An international perspective*, Guelph: Palgrave Macmillan.

DeKeseredy, W. S. (2011) *Violence against women: Myths, facts, controversies*, Toronto: University of Toronto Press.

Durfee, M., Tilton Durfee, D. and West, M. P. (2002) 'Child fatality review: an international movement', *Child Abuse and Neglect*, 26: 619–36.

Fitz-Gibbon, K. and Walklate, S. (2016) *Homicide, gender and responsibility: An international perspective*, London: Routledge.

Fregoso, R.-L. and Bejarano, C. (eds) (2010) *Terrorizing women: Feminicide in the Americas*, Durham, NC: Duke University Press.

García Marquez, G. (1981) *Crônica de una muerte anunciada [Chronicle of a death foretold],* Bogotá: Grupo Editorial Norma.

Gius, C. and Lalli, P. (2014) '"I loved her so much, but I killed her": romantic love as a representational frame for intimate partner femicide in three Italian newspapers', *Journal for Communication Studies*, 7(14): 53–75.

Glass, N., Koziol-Mclain, J., Campbell, J. and Block, C. R. (2004) Female-perpetrated femicide and attempted femicide, *Violence Against Women*, 10(6): 606–25.

Grana, S. J. (2001) 'Sociostrutural considerations of domestic femicide', *Journal of Family Violence*, 16: 421–35.

Hagemann-White, C. (1998) 'Violence without end? Some reflections on achievements, contradictions and perspectives of the feminist movement in Germany', in R. Klein (ed) *Multidisciplinary perspectives on family violence*, London: Routledge, pp 176–91.

Hart, S. D. (2008) 'Preventing violence: the role of risk assessment and management', in A. C. Baldry and F. W. Winkel (eds) *Intimate partner violence prevention and intervention: The risk assessment and management approach*, Hauppauge, NY: Nova Science, pp 7–18.

Heise, L. (1998) 'Violence against women: an integrated, ecological framework', *Violence Against Women*, 4(3): 262–90, https://www.ncbi.nlm.nih.gov/pubmed/12296014

Kelly, L. (1987) 'The continuum of sexual violence', in J. Hanmer and M. Maynard (eds) *Women, violence and social control: Explorations in sociology* (British Sociological Association Conference Volume series), London: Palgrave Macmillan, pp 46–60.

Kelly, L. (1988) *Surviving sexual violence*, Cambridge: Polity Press.

Kropp, P. R. and Hart, S. D. (2000) 'The Spousal Assault Risk Assessment (SARA) guide: reliability and validity in adult male offenders', *Law and Human Behavior*, 24(1): 101–18.

Lagarde, M. (2008) 'Antropologia, feminismo y política: violencia feminicide y derechos humanos de las mujeres', in M. Bullen and D. Mintegui (eds) (2008) *Retos teóricos e novas prácticas*, pp 209–39, https://www.ankulegi.org/wp-content/uploads/2012/03/0008Lagarde.pdf

Lagarde, M. (2010) 'Preface: Feminist keys for understanding feminicide: theoretical, political and legal construction', in R.-L. Fregoso and C. Bejarano (Eds.) (2010) Terrorizing women: Feminicide in the Americas, Durham, NC: Duke University Press, pp ix–xxvii.

Lagarde, M. (2011) Conferencia de clausura, *Revista casa de la mujer,* Edición Especial XX Aniversario, http://163.178.140.154/index. php/mujer/article/view/6816/6978

Magalhães, M. J. and Lima-Cruz, A. (2014) 'Violência simbólica contra as mulheres na arte e na vida: o caso de Susana e os Velhos' ['Symbolic violence against women in art and life: the case of Susan and the Elders'], *Faces de Eva,* 31: 73–96.

Magalhães-Dias, C. and Lobo, S. (2016) 'Changing representations of intimate partner femicides by a Portuguese newspaper (2006 and 2014): from episodic to thematic frames', *Ex Aequo,* 34: 93–108.

Meneghel, S. N. and Portella, A. P. (2017) 'Feminicídios: conceitos, tipos e cenários' ['Feminicides: concepts, types and scenarios'], *Ciência e Saúde Coletiva,* 22: 3077–86.

Meneghel, S., Ceccon, R. F., Hesler, L. Z. Margarites, A. F., Rosa, S. and Vasconcelos, V. (2013) 'Femicídios: narrativas de crimes de gênero' ['Femicides: narratives of gender crimes'], *Interface (Boucatu),* 17(46): 523–33.

Nation, M., Crusto, C., Wandersman, A., Kumpfer, K. L., Seybolt, D., Morrissey-Kane, E. and Davino, K. (2003) 'What works in prevention: principles of effective prevention programs', *American Psychologist,* 58: 449–56.

Pateman, C. (1988) *The sexual contract,* Palo Alto, CA: Stanford University Press.

Radford, J. (1992) 'Introduction', in J. Radford and D. Russell (eds) (1992) *Femicide: The politics of woman killing,* New York: Twaine Publishers, pp 3–12.

Radford, J. and Russell, D. (eds) (1992) *Femicide: The politics of woman killing,* New York: Twaine Publishers.

Romeva, R. R. (EU Rapporteur) (2013) *Femicide in the European Union and Latin America*, Euro-Latin American Parliamentary Assembly Committee on Social Affairs, Youth and Children, Human Exchanges, Education and Culture Working Document.

Rosa, F. A. and Magalhães, M. J. (2016) 'O ativismo como didática para a prevenção da violência de género na organização escolar: uma reflexão feminista e queer acerca de um projeto de intervenção no contexto português [Activism as didactics to prevent gender violence'], Atas do IX Congresso Português de Sociologia, Portugal, Território e Territórios, Lisbon: APS.

Richards, L. (2003) *Findings from the multi-agency domestic violence murder reviews in London*, London: Commander Baker Metropolitan police.

Rimsza, M. E., Schackner, R. A., Bowner, K. A. and Marshall, W. (2002) 'Can child deaths be prevented? The Arizona Child Fatality Review Progam experience', *Pediatrics*, 110: 1–7.

Sharp-Jeffs, N. and Kelly, L. (2016) *Domestic homicide review (DHR): Case analysis*, Standing Together Against Domestic Violence and London Metropolitan University, www.standingtogether.org.uk/sites/default/files/docs/STADV_DHR_Report_Final.pdf

Starfield, B., Hyde, J., Gérvas, J. and Heath, I. (2008) 'The concept of prevention: a good idea gone astray?' *Journal of Epidemiology and Community Health*, 62: v580–83.

Taylor, R. and Jasinski, J. (2011) 'Femicide and the feminist perspective', *Homicide Studies*, 15(4): 341–62.

Toledo Vásquez, Patsilí (2008) '¿Tipificar el femicidio?', *Anuário de direchos humanos*, 4: 213–19.

Watt, K. A. (2008) 'Understanding risk factors for intimate partner femicide: the role of domestic violence fatality review teams', in A. Baldry and F. Winkel (eds) *Intimate partner violence prevention and intervention* Hauppauge, NY: Nova Science, pp 44–60.

Websdale, N. (1999) *Understanding domestic homicide*, Boston, MA: Northeastern University Press.

Websdale, N. (2003) 'Reviewing domestic violence deaths', *National Institute of Justice*, 250: 26–31.

Websdale, N., Sheeran, M. and Johnson, B. (2001) *Reviewing domestic violence fatalities: Summarizing national developments*, Minneapolis, MN: Minnesota Center Against Violence and Abuse.

Webster, R. A., Schnitzer, P. G. and Jenny, C. (2003) 'Child death review: the state of the nation', *American Journal of Preventive Medicine*, 25(1): 58–64.

Wilson, M. and Daly, M. (1998) 'Lethal and nonlethal violence against wives and the evolutionary psychology of male sexual proprietariness', in, R. E. Dobash and R. P. Dobash (eds) *Sage series on violence against women, Vol. 9. Rethinking violence against women*, Thousand Oaks, CA: Sage, pp 199–230.

Wolfe, D. and Jaffe, P. (1999) 'Emerging strategies in the prevention of domestic violence', *The Future of Children*, 9: 133–44.

SIX

Exploring the data on femicide across Europe

Consuelo Corradi, Anna Costanza Baldry, Sümeyra Buran, Christiana Kouta, Monika Schröttle and Ljiljana Stevkovic

Introduction

In recent years, the notion of femicide has expanded in social, criminological and epidemiological research to grasp the basic differences underpinning the killing of a female, as opposed to a male, victim. While femicide research in Australia and the US has been a consolidated trend in criminology and feminist studies since the 1990s (Stout, 1992; Mouzos, 1999; Campbell et al, 2003; Frye et al, 2005), its development in Europe has been much more recent and represents the outcome, primarily, of top-down social pressure. The combined effect of the recent proceedings of the 'Femicide across Europe' COST network (active in 30 European countries from 2013 to 2017), together with awareness-raising by the media in many countries and the Resolution adopted by the United Nations General Assembly on 11 February 2014 (United Nations, 2014), inter alia, have acted as catalysts for change, contributing significantly to fostering femicide research in Europe. An extensive analysis of the definition of femicide is presented in Chapter 2 of this book.

Femicide is an important contributor to homicides. No systematic review exists for femicide globally, providing rates or at least accurate, country-level estimates of the killing of women 'because they are women'. There is, however, a systematic review of intimate partner homicide – this being the closest definition to femicide we can find in the scientific literature. Leading authors have estimated that, across 66 countries between 1989 and 2011, at least 14% of all murders were committed by an intimate partner, with intimate partners committing at least 39% of female and 6% of male homicide (Stöckl et al, 2013). In European countries such as Italy, Spain, Portugal or France, where female homicide rates are fairly low compared to other non-EU countries, the murder of women by former and current partners accounts for a large proportion of violent deaths among women (Corradi and Stöckl, 2014). These observations confirm the so-called 'Verkko's laws', a classic reference of European homicide research. Drawing on extensive statistical research, the Finnish scholar V. Verkko observed that the proportion of female homicide victims was higher when the overall homicide rate was low, and vice versa (Verkko, 1951, cited by Kivivuori et al, 2013).

In the same way that homicide data are considered to be 'the most valid and reliable for cross-national comparison' (Marshall and Summers, 2013: 39), we believe that femicide data constitute a highly dependable source for comparison of levels of violence against women (VAW). It is true that rates of VAW are far higher than femicide ratios in any one country, because VAW is a very widespread phenomenon, ranging from non-physical coercion to non-lethal and lethal violence against the victim. However, femicide is the area where official statistics on gender-based violence are more robust than any other data type: even if the notion of femicide is debatable, the unit of measurement is the number of female corpses. The problem arises in defining femicide operationally in such a manner as to make it comparable across countries. Data collection in Europe shows that entry fields recording the victim's age and the perpetrator's intention are the two parameters that may be preventing effective comparison of femicide databases.

In Chapter 3, the overall challenges and opportunities of data collection are discussed. In this chapter, we will review and explore in detail the data on femicide across Europe. In the following section, we present the data sources at European level. In a later section, we offer an overview of resources in 26 European countries. This constitutes the most recent and reliable exploration of data availability in single nation states. Finally, we will draft conclusions regarding the strengths and weaknesses of existing data and implications for the future of femicide research in Europe.

Data sources at the European level

Research on femicide resulting from intimate partner violence makes clear that, almost without exception, women are at greater risk than men and the homicides of women are most frequently perpetrated by male intimate partners. Studies by the United Nations Office on Drugs and Crime (UNODC) confirm two significant factors: first, that, in many countries, intimate partner or family-related homicide is the major cause of homicide against women and, second, that female homicide rates are much more likely to be driven by this type of violence than by the organized crime-related homicide typology that disproportionately affects men (United Nations Office of the High Commissioner for Human Rights, 2015). In 2012 almost half (47%) of all women murdered worldwide were killed by a family member or intimate partner, compared with 6% of male homicide victims. Femicide is also significantly undetected and underreported, since prosecutions usually do not integrate a gender perspective. There is a clear need to focus on femicide as a form of gender-based violence, and to observe and monitor the problem systematically at national and international levels.

While some countries have already developed national databases with more detailed information on the cases of femicide (for example, Italy, UK, Spain and Serbia), these national databases have not yet been collated or integrated at a European level. Indeed, to date only a few data resource collections have been implemented at the European level. Furthermore, existing data are often based purely on crime statistics, which provide very limited additional information on cases and the victim–offender relationship, or even on the gender of the victim and the perpetrator; nor is such data consistently available for every country.

The following international bodies are intending to, or have already commenced, collection of information that either focuses on or incorporates data on homicide, with a specific inclusion of the victims' gender:

- Eurostat data on homicides (based on official crime statistics)
- The European Homicide Monitor (EHM)
- UNODC's Femicide Watches
- The World Health Organization (WHO)

We review below the type of information that can be extracted from each database, and demonstrate the continuing absence of reliable and comparable data on femicide.

Eurostat data on homicides

Crime statistics are one of the most available administrative data sources across the EU member states (EIGE, 2014: 34). Eurostat's main activity is to merge statistics from different sectors, provided by the member states on a European level, and to work on harmonizing statistics. Eurostat provides crime statistics on homicides that allow access to gendered information

Table 6.1: Available crime statistics on intentional homicides of female victims aged 15+ disaggregated by country

Country code	Country	Data available		Country code	Country	Data available	
		2011	2014			2011	2014
AT	Austria	x	x	IE	Ireland		
BE	Belgium			IT	Italy	x	x
BG	Bulgaria	x	x	LT	Lithuania		
CY	Cyprus	x		LU	Luxembourg	x	
CZ	Czech Republic	x	x	LV	Latvia		x
DE	Germany	x	x	MT	Malta	x	x
DK	Denmark	x	x	NL	Netherlands	x	x
EE	Estonia		x	PL	Poland		
EL	Greece			PT	Portugal		
ES	Spain	x	x	RO	Romania		
FI	Finland	x	x	SE	Sweden		
FR	France			SI	Slovenia	x	x
HR	Croatia	x	x	SK	Slovakia		x
HU	Hungary	x	x	UK	United Kingdom	x	

Source: Eurostat, 2016b

on the number of both male and female victims of homicides aged 15 years and above. The number of intentional, completed homicides is available for all 28 EU member states (Eurostat, 2016a). The data have been compiled annually since 2008.

Table 6.1 shows for which countries Eurostat has collected data on the number of female victims of intentional, completed homicides up to 2014. About 60% of member states were able to provide gender-aggregated data for homicides in 2014.

As the Eurostat data on homicides are based on each country's national police data, it is crucial to note the availability (or absence) of gender-aggregated police statistics. According to the police data from a more recent analysis, EIGE (2017) found that 14 European countries hold available data on homicide, including the victim's sex and victim–perpetrator relationship; eight countries have data on victim's gender only; six countries have no such data (cf. Table 6.2). The availability of gender-aggregated and more detailed crime data on homicides is a rising trend.

Table 6.2: Availability of data on femicide through police statistics

Type of VAW	Availability of data including victim's sex and victim–perpetrator relationship	Data available, but no precise relationship breakdown	No available data, or no breakdown by sex of the victim
Femicide	14 (CZ, DE, ES, FR, HR, IT, LV, NL, PT, RO, SI, SK, FI, UK)	8 (BE, BG, EE, IE, CY, HU, AT, SE)	6 (DK, EL, LT, LU, MT, PL)

Source: EIGE, 2017

According to the justice statistics, EIGE (2017) found that only five European countries have available data on homicide that include the victim's sex and victim–perpetrator relationship; seven countries have data on victim's gender only; 16 countries have no such data. Thus, the police statistics will remain the central source for official statistics on femicide across Europe.

Table 6.3: Availability of data on femicide through justice statistics

Type of VAW	Availability of data including victim's sex and victim–perpetrator relationship breakdown	Data available, but no precise relationship breakdown	No available data, or no breakdown by sex of the victim
Femicide	5 (ES, FR, LT, NL, RO)	7 (EE, CY, LU, HU, PL, SE, SK)	16 (BE, BG, CZ, DK, DE, IE, EL, HR, IT, LV, MT, AT, PT, SI, FI, UK)

Source: EIGE, 2017

As crime statistics across Europe are due to be harmonized increasingly, the absence of data in the EU member states will show a tendency to improve in the coming years.

Nevertheless, it needs to be stressed that while crime statistics are a preliminary and relevant resource to measure the extent and gendered nature of crimes, they do not offer the in-depth information on the motives and background factors required to improve prevention measures or offer early intervention.

The European Homicide Monitor (EHM)

Within the European Homicide Monitor (EHM), Finland, Sweden and the Netherlands have developed a more precise and differentiated database on homicides (Granath et al, 2011: 32; Liem et al, 2013). These incorporate the legal codes for murder, manslaughter, infanticide and assault leading to death. As for the Eurostat data, attempted homicides are excluded, as are suicides, involuntary manslaughter and legally justified killings (Granath et al, 2011: 32). The database aims to include information on the gender of both victims and offenders, and collects additional background information on the cases. The EHM data set consists of 85 variables, including victim, offender and incident characteristics (Liem et al, 2013). To access the data, various sources are used and combined, such as information from the media, death statistics, police and court statistics, and other available sources. Each country is entitled to use all sources that are valid and available. The intention is to involve other European countries systematically, in order to gain a broader case basis for in-depth investigation and comparison over time and between countries (Liem, n.d.).

The EHM is based on the network of the European Homicide Research Group, coordinated by Marieke Liem from Leiden University.[1] It stipulates both research on homicides and the exchange between researchers, and has also incorporated several members of the COST Action network on femicide. It includes researchers from 19 countries (Sweden, Norway, Finland, Denmark, Germany, the Netherlands, Poland, UK, Austria, Italy, Portugal, Spain, Estonia, Switzerland, Romania, Malta, Turkey, Israel and Croatia[2]) and could offer the relevant core of researchers to be included for the new observatory on femicide across Europe.

UNODC's Femicide Watches

Various sources of data and information exist on gender-related killings. Several factors would affect the comparability of data over time. These relate primarily to the data completeness, the use of various classifications and the type of certifiers (Šimonović, 2016).

---

[1] See http://escnewsletter.org/newsletter/2016-2/european-homicide-research-group-ehrg

[2] See www.violenceresearchinitiative.org/members.html

There are several sources of information from which data could be collated and collected, each with its own specific limitations.

UNODC is leading global efforts to improve and compare crime and criminal justice data. Its report entitled *Global study on homicide 2013* (UNODC, 2013) contains a section on interpersonal homicide. The view adopted by UNODC is that, given the numerous challenges of comprehensive measurement of gender-related violence, exploring intimate partner and family-related homicide is one means of gaining a clearer understanding of the killing of women for gender-related reasons.

According to UNODC, a relevant resource for data on gender-related killings is the International Classification of Crime for Statistical Purposes, endorsed by the Statistical Commission in March 2015 and the Commission on Crime Prevention and Criminal Justice in May 2016. The Commission on Crime Prevention and Criminal Justice established an international statistical standard for data collection, drawn from both administrative records and survey-generated data. The classification adopted does not specify *crimes* but, rather, focuses on the *motivation* behind the crime. In other words, the crime classification framework is based on *behavioural* descriptions instead of legal codes. Femicide therefore falls under the classification of *intentional homicide*, namely, unlawful death inflicted upon a person with the intent to cause death or serious injury. According to the UNODC approach, three classification criteria are applied when a particular act of killing is to be classified, which further characterize the intentional homicide and can be used to define it in greater detail. These criteria are the *situational context*, the *relationship* between victim and perpetrator and the *mechanism* of killing. Situational context refers to whether the homicide takes place between two persons who had a prior relationship, or whether a homicide is related to other criminal activities or is sociopolitical in nature. Within the additional disaggregation of the relationship between the victim and perpetrator, it is recorded whether the perpetrator was an intimate partner, a family member or another person known to the victim, or if the perpetrator was unknown to the victim. Lastly, within the disaggregation of mechanism of killing, the type of weapon or other means used are similarly recorded.

As part of its work to construct the evidence database, UNODC has embarked on the strengthening of United Nations data collection systems, the development of standards for comparative justice statistics and the development of the 'global picture' of gender-related killing (UNODC, 2013: 49 and 52; UNODC, 2015: 13 and 33). Based on the recommendation of Dubravka Šimonović, the UN Special Rapporteur on violence against women, its causes and consequences, all states are invited to establish a 'femicide watch', or a 'gender-related killing of women' watch.[3]

In Šimonović's most recent report to the UN General Assembly (A/71/398) (Šimonović, 2016), the elaborated modalities for establishment of the femicide watch and/or observatory as an interdisciplinary panel of experts that collects and analyses data on femicides with the aim of preventing such incidents, are presented as follows:

(a) There should be a flexible model for the establishment of a national femicide watch that should depend on the needs and national realities of each state. Where there is no such mechanism, they should be established where there are existing systems and structures for reporting violence against women and incorporated into them (§ D.83.a).
(b) States should systematically collect relevant disaggregated data on all forms of violence against women, in particular on femicide or the gender related killing of women, which could include the killing of children in this regard. States

---

[3] See http://femicide-watch.org

should disaggregate data on femicide under two broad categories, which could include subcategories in line with their national realities, namely, intimate partner femicide or family-related femicide, based on a relationship between the victim and the perpetrator, and other femicides (§ D.83.b).

(c) States should establish a femicide watch or femicide review panels or observatories on violence against women at the global, national or regional level in order to analyse data on femicide and propose concrete measures to prevent such crimes (§ D.83.c).

(d) Femicide watch panels should be established as interdisciplinary bodies with the inclusion of legal professionals, ombudspersons and representatives of non-governmental organizations and be connected to or integrated with existing mechanisms on the prevention of violence against women, such as observatories on violence against women and bodies that monitor the implementation of national action plans on violence against women. If the panel is integrated into an existing mechanism, it should be high profile, for example, as a special unit or project (§ D.83.d).

(e) Non-governmental organizations or national human rights institutions could establish their own femicide watch reviews panels (§D.83.e).

(f) The mandate of femicide watch panels or observatories on violence against women would include systematic analyses of all cases of femicide, including court cases, with the aim of determining gaps in the response system to such violence, the criminal justice system and judicial procedures and of establishing risk factors to prevent such violence and to protect women and girls from femicide (§D.83.f).

(g) As far as possible, such femicide reviews should include suicide cases and the killing of children relating to gender-based violence against their mothers (§D.83.g).

(h) In every case, the personal information that has been provided by the victims and the family members should be incorporated only into databases with their informed consent with regard to its possible use. This information should be protected in accordance with international standards on the protection of privacy (§D.83.h).

These aims for further data collection are highly relevant for the establishment of the European Observatory on Femicide, which is discussed in more detail in the following chapter.

World Health Organization (WHO)

WHO collects data on multiple causes of violence and injury-related deaths, as well as statistics on different forms of violence. With regard to homicide, it reports data divided according to the gender of the victim, but no data are provided on the type of relationship or gender of the perpetrator.[4] Thus, the data based on the national death statistics are essentially incomplete and could not serve as the central source for data collection on femicide. In addition, the data are not directly compatible with crime statistics and it is problematic to decide which source holds greater validity. This could provide incentive to focus rather on crime statistics and/or on a range of other sources.

Overview of resources in 26 European countries

One of the aims of the COST Action IS1206, 'Femicide across Europe', was to assess the feasibility of building a European Observatory on Femicide. What follows is a census of the resources that are available today at country level in 26 European countries according to the national experts of the

---

[4]   See http://apps.who.int/violence-info/homicide

COST Action research network.[5] We are deeply convinced that building a European observatory is possible and that this should be undertaken in close partnership with the many institutions, NGOs, and public and private research centres that engage daily in collecting, classifying and disseminating data on femicide across Europe. We believe that there are many country-level resources that can be implemented towards this goal today. Femicide research is no longer in its infancy. Country-level resources are unconnected and extremely varied, but they provide the starting point for a European observatory.

1. Austria (by Birgitt Haller)

1.1 Definition

There is no specific term in German for the murder of women: the same expression is used for both female and male victims (the German word *Mord* is of Germanic origin and does not allow for a female suffix). The intervention centres (victim protection organizations, established by the Austrian Protection against Violence Act 1997) have pointed out the risk of being killed by a (former) partner for many years.

1.2 Resources

The first (and only) empirical research study on femicide was completed by Birgitt Haller in 2011, financed by the Ministry of Women's Affairs. Under the title of 'High-risk victims. Homicide in relationships', all convictions for (attempted) femicide from 2008 to 2010 were analysed: 39 legal proceedings against male perpetrators (as well as eight legal proceedings against female aggressors) (Haller, 2014).

---

[5] Information from the country experts and EIGE's reports might differ due to different information sources.

Homicide data based on police reports are collected and published annually by the Austrian Police/ Ministry of the Interior. Therefore, for example, it may emerge that a person was not murdered, but died as a result of a domestic accident. Police data provide the sex of both victim and aggressor, but the categories used to define the relationship between victim and aggressor are very imprecise: they reflect whether the persons concerned had been living together or not, but do not reveal the type of relationship between them (partners, aunt and niece and so on). Therefore, precise information on femicide in the strict sense is not available.

2. Croatia (by Ivana Radacic and Irena Cajner Mraovic)
2.1 Definition

The notion of femicide has been in circulation in Croatia since the late 1990s but mainly among the research community. Although there are several studies of domestic violence in Croatia, the first paper to use the concept of femicide was published in 2014 (Asančaić, 2014). The term femicide is not widely used in Croatia; rather, most reliable sources use expressions such as 'killing of women'. The expression 'intimate homicide' is also used to indicate the killing of a woman by an intimate partner as a specific form of homicide.

The term femicide is most commonly used by feminist web portals, which occasionally publish articles about the problem of intimate partner violence in Croatia and report the developments with respect to femicide within the UN or in other countries. Government bodies do not employ this term.

2.2 Resources

There are no comprehensive resources on femicide in Croatia. The Ministry of the Interior is the body that officially collects data on reported murders of women, which include information about the victim's relationship with the perpetrator, but not necessarily the motivation or the context in which the murder occurred. Conversely, publicly available data reported in the Statistical Overview of the Basic Security Indicators and Police Work Results, published annually on the ministry's website, contain only information about the sex of the perpetrators and the victims of homicide. The annual publication *Men and women in Croatia,* published by the Croatian Bureau of Statistics does not contain any data on femicide.

3. Cyprus (by Christiana Kouta and Elena Rousou)
3.1 Definition

There is no legal definition of femicide in Cyprus. While the murder of a woman or a girl by a family member is recognized in law, it is only in relation to family violence (Violence in the Family Law), which is not gender-specific. Under section 3 of the Violence in the Family (Prevention and Protection of Victims) Laws 119(I)/2000 and 212(I)/2004, this refers to 'any act, omission or behavior, which causes physical, sexual or mental injury to any member of the family and includes violence used for the purpose of having sexual intercourse without the consent of the victim as well as of restricting its freedom'.

When a woman or a girl is murdered by a family member, it is defined by the law as 'violence in the family', and there is no differentiation between female and male perpetrators. Homicides that take place outside the family as a result of gender-based violence (for example, by a boyfriend), are not categorized as violence against women or gender-based violence, despite the fact that analysis of the data in Cyprus demonstrates that the majority of these cases can indeed be categorized as gender-based violence and acts of femicide.

3.2 Resources

No forums and limited literature related to the issue of femicide exists in Cyprus. On the other hand, there are organizations dealing with family violence, although those organizations are not gender specific:

1. **The Service for Families and Children (Social Welfare Services):** This aims to support the family unit, in order to enable family members to perform their roles and responsibilities effectively, to resolve family disputes that threaten the unity of family, to safeguard the protection and the welfare of children, to prevent delinquent behaviour and domestic violence, and to encourage the rehabilitation of people involved in antisocial behaviour and delinquency.[6]

2. **The Police Crime Combatting Department (Domestic Violence and Child Abuse Office):** This attends to all matters dealing with prevention, repression and handling of domestic violence and child abuse.[7]

3. **The Association for the Prevention and Handling of Violence in the Family:** This is a national centre providing preventative services for domestic violence, supporting and protecting receivers of violence.[8]

---

[6] See www.mlsi.gov.cy/mlsi/mlsi.nsf/mlsi14_en/mlsi14_en?OpenDocument

[7] See www.police.gov.cy/police/police.nsf/dmldept3_en/dmldept3_en?OpenDocument

[8] See www.domviolence.org.cy/?lang=EN&cat=0 See further: Advisory Committee for the Prevention of and Combatting Violence in the Family: www.familyviolence.gov.cy; *Cyprus Mail* (2014) 'Stop violence against women, June 23: http://cyprus-mail.com/2014/06/23/more-than-30-women-murdered-in-cyprus-in-past-nine-years; Kapardis et al, 2017, and Kyriakidou, 2012;.Violence in the Family (Prevention and Protection of Victims) Laws 119(I)/2000 and 212(I)/2004: www.cylaw.org/nomoi/enop/ind/2000_1_119/section-scec2be7aa-7418-4ef2-ac1e-9683797b3690-ai4f3e06ce1acd5.html

4. Denmark (by Yvonne Mørck)

4.1 Definition

Until a few years ago, the term 'wife killing', or 'wife homicide', was employed in the judicial system (and was linked to marital status), but this has now changed to 'partner killing' (unlinked to marital status or gender), that is, it is a gender-neutral concept. The notion of femicide is not used in the official Danish system for crime registration. However, victim statistics regarding homicide are divided by gender (Statistics Denmark). The term femicide is used to some extent in the Danish media.

5. France (by Lisa Anteby-Jemini and Valérie Raffin)

5.1 Definition

The concept of femicide (in French, *fémicide* or *féminicide*) is rarely utilized in France. In this country, the media reports of femicide cases by an intimate partner generally conceal the violence and the murder, by denoting them as 'family dramas' or 'separation dramas'. In many official documents the term *homicide conjugal* (marital homicide) is used instead of *fémicide conjugal* (marital femicide), for example. However, since 2014 the word *féminicide* has entered the *French Petit Robert Dictionary*, and is defined as 'the murder of a woman or a girl because she is a woman'. The common term used to refer to these murders in the official reports is 'victims of marital violence', and the Ministry of the Interior's annual national report on the number of deaths defines them as 'violent deaths in the couple'. The last survey, called VIRAGE (violence and gender relations), begun in 2000, recently published its results, but still refers to femicide as 'acts of violence against women', including cases of murder (Hamel et al, 2016). An association named Osez le féminisme

(Don't be shy about feminism) has been actively advocating for the legal recognition of the term since 2014.[9]

5.2 Resources

In official reports in France, 'violence within the couple' is a term applied not only to the murder of women by their intimate partner (husband, ex-husband, lover, boyfriend or potential boyfriend, whether there have been sexual relations or not), but also to the murder of men by their female partners, murders by same-sex partners, the suicides of perpetrators (for which, given the lack of police data, one can only offer an estimate) and homicides qualified as 'collateral victims' (that is, children, family members or others who tried to interpose themselves, such as parents, neighbours, lawyers and so on). The data also includes estimates for the number of suicides resulting from marital violence, irrespective of whether this refers to the suicide of the victim or the perpetrator (Jaspard, 2005). The data also includes further criteria, such as the region of France, French or foreign nationality, possible cause of murder and so on, in relation to both the victim and the perpetrator.

The data for the number of suicides of women victims of domestic violence is still absent in statistics for Europe. In France, for example, a rate of 13% has been applied to the national rate for suicides in order to estimate the number of real suicides resulting from violence within the couple. This rate was derived from the National Survey on Violence against Women.

The annual report on data for violent partner deaths appears on both the website of the French Ministry of the Interior – through its Delegation for Victims (DAV) – and the website of the French Ministry for Families, Childhood and Women's

---

[9] See https://reconnaissonslefeminicide.olf.site

Rights.[10] Official action and responses are conducted through MIPROF (the Inter-ministerial Mission for the Protection of Women against Violence and the Fight against the Trafficking of Human Beings).

There is a National Observatory of Violence against Women, which also publishes statistical reports on VAW drawn from the results of INSEE surveys on 'Life Framework and Security' (CVS).[11]

In addition, there are a number of local observatories, for example, in the Greater Paris region and in the region of Seine-Saint-Denis.[12] Data is available on homicides and violence leading to a death in a couple (including the murder of children and collaterals). The average figure for deaths in couples in France between 2006 and 2013 is 205 deaths (Attané et al, 2015), including:

- 159 femicides in heterosexual couples;
- 29 husband deaths in heterosexual couples;
- 2 husband deaths in gay couples;
- 1 femicide in a lesbian couple;
- 9 murders of children;
- 5 collateral murders;
- 54 suicides of male perpetrators.

There have been only very slight variations in these figures over the last 10 years in France, and these represent 30% of the total number of homicides and violence that led to death in

---

[10] The most recent report can be found at www.familles-enfance-droitsdesfemmes.gouv.fr/parution-du-rapport-annuel-concernant-les-morts-violentes-au-sein-du-couple

[11] See http://stop-violences-femmes.gouv.fr/IMG/pdf/Lettre_ONVF_8_-_Violences_faites_aux_femmes_principales_donnees_-_nov15.pdf

[12] See www.centre-hubertine-auclert.fr/observatoire-regional-des-violences-faites-aux-femmes and https://www.seine-saint-denis.fr/-Observatoire-des-violences-envers-les-femmes-.html

2013, whereas the proportion of violent deaths related to other circumstances has fallen.

6. Georgia (by Tiko Tsomaia)

According to a global study on homicide conducted in 2013, the intentional homicide rate per 100,000 population is 3.4, which puts Georgia in the group of low homicide rate countries. The percentage of male and female intentional homicide victims is 75.7% and 24.3%, respectively.

According to the analysis provided by the Chief Prosecutor's Office of Georgia, 53 women were killed in 2014/15, of whom 27 cases were denoted as 'domestic violence murders' and 18 were killed by their intimate partners.

6.1 Definition

The term femicide has been used regularly by the media, activists and the general public since 2014. This term entered public discourse after a murder that occurred on 17 October 2014, when a man recently released from prison killed his ex-wife and then committed suicide in front of students and professors at Ilia State University in Tbilisi, Georgia. The broad media coverage of this particular murder and other killings of women in 2014 brought femicide to the foreground and caused a public outcry. Different organizations (NGOs, media, academia and state institutions) define femicide as the gender-related killing of women, related to gender-based violence by an intimate partner.

6.2 Resources

Legislation in the Republic of Georgia does not recognize femicide as a separate crime; all cases of killings of women are investigated and punished as crimes against human beings.

Therefore, no separate statistics are collected on the killings of women based on gender.

Currently, femicide cases are investigated under penal code articles, including murder, murder in aggravating circumstances, intentional murder in a state of sudden strong emotional excitement, intentional infliction of grave injury that caused death, incitement to suicide, an article specifying domestic crimes and articles that describe the commission of a crime related to sex.

Journalists and civil society can only speculate about the veracity of the data, since government institutions and legislation have not responded to requests for detailed crime data, which would help shed light on the actual trends. Government institutions (the Ministry of the Interior, the Prosecutor's Office and the courts) remain the source for the collection and dissemination of data. No organization exists to collect and collate data from alternative sources and double-check the information.

There are a number of groups following the topic:

1. The Georgian Institute of Public Affairs (GIPA) has received a grant from the European Commission to track violent crime against women.[13]
2. In 2015 the Public Prosecutor's Office published an analysis of intimate and family homicide.[14]
3. On 4 April 2016 the Georgian Young Lawyers Association released a study entitled 'Judgments in cases of femicide – 2014'.[15]
4. The Public Defender of Georgia publishes special reports.[16]

---

[13] See http://newscafe.ge/homicide/Honor_killing.html

[14] See http://pog.gov.ge/geo/news?info_id=890

[15] See https://gyla.ge/en/post/kvlevis-prezentacia-femicidis-saqmeebis-ganachenebi-2014

[16] See www.ombudsman.ge/en/reports/specialuri-angarishebi

5. The United Nations Population Fund (UNFPA) is paying attention to one particular type of femicide: sex-selective abortions.[17]

6. The Georgian Center for Psychosocial and Medical Rehabilitation of Torture Victims (GCRT) works with victims of gender-based violence.[18]

7. Germany (by Monika Schröttle and Ksenia Meshkova)

7.1 Definition

The term femicide is not widely used in Germany. One possible reason might be its similarity to 'genocide' and its connotations for German history. Nevertheless, the killings of women are recognized as an extreme form of VAW and are included in criminological data and murder statistics; they are also recognized in research and policies on VAW. There are few publications and studies focusing on femicide. The most recent systematic work was a research study carried out by Luise Greuel (Greuel, 2009) on the escalation of violence in intimate partner relationships. In addition, Heynen and Zahradnik (2017) have conducted a research project on homicide within families in the context of intimate partner violence, where relatives were interviewed about the circumstances and consequences of the homicides in a systematic manner.

In order to facilitate the collection of data on femicide, it is first crucial to include all cases related to the killing of women. Gender-based cases can then be filtered out according to the victim–perpetrator relationship (for example, the killing of a woman by an intimate partner). The term 'partner' can be defined in broad terms to include those who are married and

---

[17] See www.unfpa.org/gender-biased-sex-selection

[18] See http://gcrt.ge/en

unmarried, cohabiting/non-cohabiting relationships, and dating partners.

7.2 Resources

There are three bodies that collect femicide data in Germany on a regular basis. However, two of them (that is, with the exception of the police) are neither financed nor institutionalized:

- The German Police Criminological Statistics (PKS) collects all cases of killings (including additional data on the gender of the victims and victim–perpetrator relationship). Thus, the number of women killed and – to some extent – the relationship to the perpetrator can be accessed. Another available source is the court statistics on convicted perpetrators. One remaining problem is that court statistics are not integrated with police statistics.[19]
- Over the past few years, The Network of Autonomous Shelters (ZIF) has collected reports about cases of femicide via internet searches alongside the published data from the police and the media. This information is collected for internal purposes and has not been published regularly to date.
- In 2016 two researchers from the Institute for Empirical Sociological Research at the University of Nuremberg (Monika Schröttle and Julia Habermann) began systematically collecting information and data on femicides and building a national database. They also joined the European Homicide Monitor (Granath et al, 2011) and are planning to institutionalize this project within the framework of a national scientific monitor under the Istanbul Convention and VAW, in cooperation with the German Ministry for Women and Family Affairs.

---

[19] See www.bka.de/DE/AktuelleInformationen/StatistikenLagebilder/ PolizeilicheKriminalstatistik/PKS2015/pks2015_node.html

8. Greece (by Athena Peglidou)

8.1 Definition

The term femicide (γυναικοκτονία-*gynaikoktonia*) is not in use, even in media discourse, where these murders are described mostly as a 'family tragedy', 'crime of passion', 'love crime' or even 'unexpected crime', in which the 'unfortunate woman' lost her life.

8.2 Resources

There is no statistical data in Greece concerning the female death rate as a result of assault, because data on homicides are not sex-disaggregated. According to the Greek Police Statistical Service, the only available quantitative data concern the sex of the perpetrator or the victim and the locus of murder. Tables 6.4 and 6.5 show the figures for 2013 according to the victims' sex and murder loci and according to the perpetrators' sex and murder loci.

Table 6.4: Number of murders in Greece in 2013 according to the victim's sex and murder loci

Loci	Men	Women
Other spaces	54	9
Home	49	42
Total	103	51

Table 6.5: Number of murders in Greece in 2013 according to the perpetrator's sex and murder loci

Loci	Men	Women
Other spaces	80	2
Home	76	14
Total	156	16

The dominant femicide pattern is that of intimate partner murder. A representative case study might be a young man who has killed his girlfriend or wife because of his own excessive jealousy, perhaps after she attempted to break up their relationship. After reviewing journalistic records of the last ten years, two particular characteristics are worth mentioning: the cruelty and, in some cases, dismemberment and disappearance of the female body, as well as the suicide or attempted suicide of the perpetrator after the murder.

9. Iceland (by Freidis Freysteinsdottir and Halldora Gunnarsdottir)
9.1 Definition

Femicide as a concept has hardly gained any ground in Iceland. The term has only recently come into public use by the Icelandic members of the COST project on femicide. There has been a debate by professionals in Iceland about what the proper translation of the word should be. In reliable sources, femicide is defined as 'the killing of a woman because she is a woman by an intimate partner'. 'Partner' is defined in a broad manner, to include a husband, living and dating partner or lover; a former husband, former partner and former lovers are also included under the definition. The expression 'family femicide' is also used to designate killing by a relative, such as a father, son or other. Other cases might be included, such as so-called crimes of passion, where the perpetrator kills someone other than his partner, former partner or lover, but the victim is a woman and the motive is related to his relationship with a woman (see Freysteinsdóttir, 2017).

9.2 Resources

Data on femicide, as such, are not collected in Iceland. However, three databases with information on murders provide the possibility to generate data on femicide in Iceland:

- Police data: The police keep a closed database on all crimes, including murders. This database may be consulted on request, but there is no guarantee of provision of access to the data for research use.
- Open source data: On Icelandic Wikipedia, a list of murders going back centuries can be accessed. The list was created according to word of mouth information and is maintained by a lawyer. However, not all murder cases, including cases of femicide, appear on that list and the term 'femicide' is not used.
- A database called Fons juris:[20] This is not public, but private; people are required to pay for access to data therein. This database includes all verdicts issued in Iceland from 1920 and has been published electronically. Cases of femicide are retrievable from the database, under a legal definition of the crime of murder in the General Criminal Law [Almenn hegningarlög] No. 19/1940 (§ 211) and severe physical assault (para. 218), which could include assaults that result in death. This database does not include cases dismissed for lack of evidence, although there might be a suspicion that a murder or femicide has occurred. Those types of cases are not included in verdicts.

Ireland (by Siobán O'Brien Green)
10.1 Definition

The word femicide is rarely used in Ireland and does not appear in recent and relevant statutory national policy or guideline documents, or in the Irish Statute Book (a collection of Irish legislation). The terms 'female homicide', 'intimate partner homicide' or 'homicide/murder' are used. Holt defines femicide as 'the killing of a woman by her intimate partner or ex-partner' (Holt, 2007).

---

[20] http://fonsjuris.is

10.2 Resources

Data on femicide in Ireland are, or could potentially be, available from the following sources:

1. **Central Statistics Office – An Garda Síochána (Irish police force):** Crime statistics are collected via the PULSE (Police Using Leading Systems Effectively) system and are collated and published by the Central Statistics Office (CSO), Crime and Justice section, on a regular basis. Data from annual homicide offences can be disaggregated by sex of victim. At the time of writing (November 2017), homicide data cannot be disaggregated by sex of perpetrator and relationship of homicide victim to perpetrator; however, it is anticipated that this will change in the near future. Currently there is a review of all homicide cases in Ireland from 2003 to 2017 occurring by a team in An Garda Síochána.

2. **Coroners' Courts:** In all cases of homicide an inquest is held by the relevant coroner. Data on number of deaths reported, post mortems and inquests held are reported on an annual basis by each Coroner's Office in Ireland; these are then collated into nationwide statistics by the Coroner Service Implementation Team (CSIT). At the time of writing (November 2017), these statistics are not disaggregated by sex of the deceased or relationship of the deceased to anyone involved in the homicide. As a result, data in relation to femicide are not yet available through national CSIT statistics.

3. **Courts Service:** Murder court cases in Ireland are held in the Central Criminal Court. It is possible to conduct a review of relevant murder trial proceedings and sentencing through information on the Courts Service website in order to determine cases of femicide. However, this data is not being collated as femicide statistics.

4. **Maternal Death Enquiry:** Data on all maternal deaths (deaths during pregnancy and up to one year post-partum)

are collected and analysed by the Confidential Maternal Death Enquiry, Ireland Office (MDE). Deaths as a result of femicide during this time period are included in this data analysis and classified as 'indirect deaths'. Data from Ireland are collated with data from England, Scotland, Wales and Northern Ireland, and published as triennial reports by MBRRACE-UK. Where known, the perpetrator of the homicide is documented as family member, stranger or (ex) partner in the MBRRACE reports (Knight et al, 2015).

5. **Women's Aid Femicide Monitoring Project:** Women's Aid is an Irish domestic violence nongovernmental organisation (NGO) which has been collating media-reported cases of femicide in Ireland since 1996.[21] The project reports on the number of women murdered, location of murder, sex of perpetrator and relationship of the victim to the perpetrator, where known. Additional data, such as the victim's age, method of killing, case status (awaiting trial, case resolved and so on) and whether the case was a murder-suicide, are also collected, where known.

Israel (by Yifat Bitton and Shalva Weil)

11.1 Definition

The notion of femicide, as such, is practically absent from Israel. In recent years, however, an awareness of 'the murder of women', or 'women's murder', by their (generally) male family members is well evident in public discourse. Overall, the media in Israel plays a key role in disseminating the notion of 'women's murder' as a social phenomenon that should be condemned. In addition, Israeli academics are among the leading scholars in the field of femicide. Nowadays, it is widely accepted that the murder of women by their family members warrants special attention.

---

[21] See https://www.womensaid.ie/about/policy/natintstats.html

The criminal code assigns no specific clause to femicide, and femicide murderers are charged with the general offence of murder. In other reliable sources, femicide is mainly associated with the killing of a woman by an intimate partner, broadly defined. Highly prevalent, too, is the expression 'family honour killing', used to indicate murder by a partner or a relative on the grounds that a woman has manifested disrespect of her family by her unacceptable behaviour. This type of femicide is perceived as a category on its own and is ultimately associated with killing a woman 'due to her gender'.

11.2 Resources

Until 2012, apart from sporadic media-initiated projects, there had been no data collection available for femicide in Israel. At that time, the Parliamentary Committee on Women's Rights initiated a special report on VAW, which determined that femicide would be reported annually (Mizrahi-Simon, 2016). Despite being accessible to the public, only meagre efforts were made to disseminate this report outside the Israeli parliament, the Knesset. Since 2015, there have been no systematic, formal data on femicide in Israel – only a statement issued by the Knesset, collating statistics it claims as sourced from the Israel Police,[22] although they differed from those actually reported by the police.

In addition, in its annual report on violence, the Israel Ministry for Internal Security currently features a specific and distinct section on female victims of murder. However, no special attention is allocated to the motives underlying the murder of these women, while the report itself is laconic in tone and de-contextualized in relation to the topic. Another example of this disregard occurs in the Israel Police's official Report on Violence for 2014. The report introduces no less than nine different types

---

[22] www.knesset.gov.il/mmm/data/pdf/m03849.pdf

and definitions for murder, none of which relates specifically to the murder of women.

Academic articles on femicide in Israel have identified killings among particular ethnic groups, such as Ethiopian immigrants (Weil, 2016), Russian immigrants under the influence of alcohol (Sela-Shayovitz, 2010a) or Arab/Palestinian populations (Shalhoub-Kevorkian and Daher-Nashif, 2013) among whom the authors attribute 'honour killings' to the Occupation; intimate partner femicide, often committed with a firearm, significantly increased among immigrants during the Second Intifada (Sela-Shayovitz, 2010b). In addition, 10% of all femicides have been perpetrated among elderly women over the age of 60 in the past decade (Weil, 2017).

12. Italy (by Anna C. Baldry, Consuelo Corradi and Augusto Gnisci)
12.1 Definition

The notion of femicide has circulated in Italy since 2004, when the European SARA project and subsequently the FEAR project (both funded by the Daphne Framework) were implemented, with both addressing the killing of women due to their gender and assessment of the risk of escalation of lethal violence. As a result of these projects, publications (Baldry and Ferraro, 2008; Baldry, 2016) and conferences have disseminated the term since 2005. In 2008 B. Spinelli authored a book titled *Femminicidio* (Spinelli, 2008).

For the past decade, due to social, political and NGO movements, the term has been employed intensively, and even exploited by the media, with the aim of raising awareness on the topic. In 2012, due to the high number of femicides, there was also a political and media debate about the opportunity to have a specific category of homicide called 'femicide', which was soon deemed as raising anticonstitutional issues. Debates are still ongoing as to whether the term should be used, or if there should even be a 'dedicated' legal term identifying these crimes. Attention peaks on specific dates in the year (8 March, International Women's Day, and 25 November, International Day for the Elimination of Violence Against Women), when most of the media adress the issue and conferences are organized. Since, in Italy one femicide occurs on average every three or four days, news media coverage of the crime responds cyclically. Social perceptions of the rates of VAW have been shaped by these waves of media response, together with social and political attention.

In actual fact, for the past five to ten years, the number of women killed due to femicide has remained constant (at approximately 100 per year), while the trend for overall homicides has fallen: this is despite the fact that policies and strategies for prevention have supposedly been put in place.

In 2013, Law No. 119, referred to also as the 'Law on Femicide', although it is not technically such, was passed. It introduced a set of criminal interventions into the Italian criminal justice system, focusing on additional suppressive powers for the police and legal authorities for intervention in protection of victims and to decrease the risk of recidivism. Several provisions were brought to reduce the number of cases of femicide and address domestic violence in general; others were introduced in accordance with proposals set out under the so-called Istanbul Convention, which was also ratified by Italy and put in place in August 2014, as an abiding law. The provisions set out in the 119/2013 law, which also introduces a biennial National Plan to prevent and combat VAW, do not specifically address femicide, but establish the foundations for its prevention. Through an extensive set of procedures, including financial support, it is producing a visible reduction in the numbers of women killed annually in Italy; however, there are clear indications that these changes are considered to be 'emergency' responses and not structured measures leading to more effective and long-term impact.

In January 2017, the Senate of the Italian Republic set up the parliamentary committee on femicide, formed by 20 senators from all parties, with the aim of identifying what is needed to stop and prevent femicide. In addition, a special law was also enacted addressing assistance to the orphans of these crimes, providing specific and dedicated support to reduce the consequences of trauma.

Femicide, although not used in the legal framework, is best defined as the killing of a woman because of her gender. Most cases relate to killing by an intimate partner. However, other killings of women might also fall under this category (for example, a woman who is raped and then killed, an exploited woman or prostitute who is killed, other family-related murders). The term 'partner' or 'ex-partner' includes the current or a previous husband, living and dating partner, lover or occasional partner. The expression 'family femicide' is also utilized to indicate killing by a relative, such as a father, son or other (Baldry et al, 2011; Corradi and Piacenti, 2016).

12.2 Resources

In view of the fact that the definition of femicide is not always consistent between agencies and social contexts in relation to calculating the number of victims, differences could also emerge. With this limit in mind, we can identify four bodies in Italy that collect data on the gender-related killing of women in the country:

1. The most accurate and longest-standing database on femicide is gathered by EURES (Economic and Social Research Centre). Since 1990, this private research centre has been collecting data from media sources on voluntary homicide and validating this information against the Ministry of the Interior source that releases official data at the end of each year. Since 2000, EURES has also focused on femicide through the

systematic collection of an extensive number of variables (inter alia: age, marital status, education, employment and so on) related to both the victim and the perpetrator (Piacenti and Pasquali, 2014).

2. Casa delle donne per non subire violenza (a women's shelter) in Bologna is one of the National Networks of DiRe shelters. This is an independent, women's only NGO, established in the 1980s and aimed at preventing and eliminating all forms of VAW. It publishes and annotates data, but this activity does not appear to be a continuous endeavour.[23]

3. Since 2014, the Ministry of the Interior has published annually a short report on intimate and family homicide.

4. The National Institute of Statistics (ISTAT) gathers data on homicide, based on data from the Ministry of Justice and the Ministry of the Interior. On 25 November 2016, ISTAT and the Department of Equal Opportunities signed an agreement to set aims for systematic data collection according to the provisions of the Istanbul Convention, including joint action with other relevant ministries (Interior and Justice) to gather data on femicide.

5. The national newspaper *Corriere della Sera* in the section '27ora' has a special online census, providing a constant update of the women killed in Italy.[24]

13. Lithuania (by Vilana Pilinkaité)
13.1 Definition

Femicide as a consequence of intimate partner violence has been mainly utilized by women's NGOs, which advocate for legal reform and policy changes in Lithuania. The term 'femicide' is rarely used in academic research. However, femicide might be retrievable under Art. 129 of the Penal Code, which identifies

---

[23] See www.casadonne.it
[24] https://27esimaora.corriere.it/la-strage-delle-donne/

sentences in cases of homicide. The same article defines the relationships between an offender and victim, in terms of close relative or family member.

13.2 Resources

Data on femicide are generally collected under statistics for homicide. The most reliable source on femicide is the register of crime statistics collected by the Ministry of the Interior. The Department of Information Technology and Communications (DITC), within the Ministry of the Interior, collects data nationally and manages its collection and systematization. Data includes cases of crimes, victims and offenders, as well as the inception of pre-trial investigation under the Penal Code. Records from police, prosecutors and judges of private prosecution cases are supposed to appear in this register. The national standard for recording administrative data is the Order of the Minister of the Interior on Regulations of the Institutional Register of Criminal Acts (*LR Vidaus reikalų ministro įsakymas 'Nusiklatimo veikų žinybinio reigstro nuostatai'*). The DITC refers to the collected administrative data to generate the statistics for crimes. It is possible to identify the numbers of victims and offenders according to gender and family relations from these crime statistics. The DITC manages the database on all pre-trial investigations, in accordance with the Penal Code. Crimes reported by the police to the judicial system include data on homicides by sex of the victim and family relations. Thus, statistics on femicide are identifiable. The DITC publishes these statistics on a specially designated website for VAW, operated by the Ministry of the Interior.[25]

---

[25] See www.bukstipri.lt/en/index.html

14. Republic of Macedonia (by Biljana Chavkoska and Viktorija Chavkoska)

14.1 Definition

In the Republic of Macedonia, there is no legally binding definition of femicide in the legal acts. The definition of homicide is covered under criminal law. Criminal law provides for a more severe sentence if the act of murder is perpetrated as family violence, so that the minimum sentence in this instance would be 10 years up to life imprisonment.[26] A new law was adopted as a *lex specialis* law, for the prevention and elimination of and protection from domestic violence, and came into force on 1 January 2015.[27] This law regulates the legal procedure for the protection and elimination of family violence, such as the legal protection of the victims of domestic violence and the obligatory activities of state institutions and civil society. The law provides definitions of family violence but does not define family violence as gender-based violence, while women and girls are not recognized as a vulnerable group. The Republic of Macedonia has a legal obligation to improve the data system for collecting information on family violence since adopting the law. Unfortunately, this is not the case in practice. Furthermore, there is no official oversight of the implementation of the law. It is expected that data resources on femicide and family violence will be improved in relation to implementation of Article 11 of the Istanbul Convention (signed in 2011) after it is ratified by parliament.

14.2 Resources

The statistical data for femicide can be obtained as follows:

---

[26] See the Criminal Code of the Republic of Macedonia, Official Gazetta, No. 19/2004

[27] See the Law on Protection from and Prevention of Family Violence, Official Gazetta, No. 138/2014

1. Through the Ministry of Internal Affairs' general report on homicide data statistics. This report renders the issue of femicide invisible, although it is reported that men are perpetrators of the murder of women. In terms of the motives for committing the murders, most are reported as occurring within the family circle and being caused by disrupted family relationships, with mostly women as victims. Due to the percentage of the female victims, it can be conclusively deduced that family violence is gender-based violence.

2. Some statistical data on femicide can be obtained from the Ministry of Labour and Social Affairs through the National Strategy for Preventing Family Violence and Homicide, as the most extreme form of family violence. However, the data for femicide is not visibly delineated, despite the fact that the statistics clearly show most of the victims to be female partners. The existing IT monitoring system for LIRICUS social services is not updated regularly, due mainly to the lack of qualified workers and equipment. By law, every citizen is legally obligated to report family violence to police officers, the centre for social work or the national SOS call line. A penalty fine of up to 1,000 euros is stipulated for citizens who fail to report incidents of family violence.

3. Unfortunately, at the present time, femicide statistics are also not covered by the National Statistics Authority, due to lack of research and official information. According to the non-official data collected by civic associations in the period from 2001 to 2016, 32 femicides were registered in the Republic of Macedonia, with 15 of these occurring in the period from 2013 to 2016.

15. Malta (by Marceline Naudi and Katya Unah)
15.1 Definition

There is no official definition of femicide in the Criminal Code.

15.2 Resources

To date, Malta does not have an official body/entity which collects femicide data, other than the police, who classify it as homicide. On request, the police can provide brief statistical information on all intentional homicides of women. The Commission on Domestic Violence collects newspaper articles following the murder of a woman. For example, in the year 2016, there were two such deaths in Malta: one in July and another in September.

Malta ratified the Istanbul Convention in 2014 and a law to ensure proper implementation was finally enacted in April 2018. The law includes the setting up of a body that is now responsible for collecting and collating all relevant data, which should include data on femicide.

16. The Netherlands (by Marieke Liem)

16.1 Definition

Femicides are not classified separately, as such, in the Netherlands. The available data allow for the extraction of female victims among sexual homicides, intimate partner homicides and other types of homicides.

16.2 Resources

In recent years (from 2003 onwards), in the Netherlands, homicides have been classified according to the Dutch Homicide Monitor (Granath et al, 2011).[28] This monitor is based on various partially overlapping sources, which also complement one another:

---

[28] For details on the construction of the dataset and the available variables, see Granath et al (2011).

1. All homicide-related newspaper articles generated by the Netherlands National News Agency (ANP): These articles contain a great deal of information on the characteristics of the homicides, perpetrators and victims.
2. The Elsevier Annual Report: *Elsevier* is a weekly magazine that publishes an annual report on all occurring homicides. This report is based on both ANP articles and police files.
3. Data stemming from police records in the Netherlands' 10 police districts: Several police districts supply (additional) data from their own documentation, which is then incorporated into the database.
4. Files from the Public Prosecution Service of the Ministry of Justice: This database includes the judicial procedures for prosecuted homicide perpetrators.

Norway (by Anne Ryen)
17.1 Definition

The Norwegian term used in official documents is *partnerdrap* ('partner murder' or 'partner killing') as well as *kvinnedrap* ('woman killing'), which is a wider and, in this context, less precise concept. 'Femicide' is an unfamiliar term in Norwegian. *Partnerdrap* implies that the victim and the partner were married, cohabitant or had a registered partnership at the time of, or prior to, the killing. The data show the victim (women-dominated) and murderer (male-dominated) by gender. Norwegian statistics include separated and divorced partners, former cohabitants and former partners, but excludes lovers who have never lived together.

17.2 Resources

Partnerdrap has been reported since 1990, and in 1998 the Norwegian government initiated research on the topic. The Kompetansesenteret for sikkerhets-, fengsels-, og rettspsykiatri, the Statutory Centre for Security, Prisons and Forensic Psychiatry at Ullevål University Hospital, was appointed as the institution responsible for research. As part of the governmental Plan of Action, a doctoral study on intimate partner violence entitled 'Vendepunkt' ('Turning Point') mapped all partner killings in the period 1980–2008, with subsequent follow-up studies and practical manuals (Vatnar, 2009 and 2015).[29] Norway issues annual national statistics on murder, including *partnerdrap*, drawn from Kripos (Norway's National Criminal Investigation Service) and police crime records in conjunction with the SSP (Central Criminal and Police Enlightenment Information Register). These statistics offer a detailed overview and are similarly reflective of trends from international studies, in that they incorporate details about previous violence and repetitive violence prior to the murder. This work has sparked a concerted endeavour to develop and formulate a policy to help prevent partner killings.[30]

Media reports have helped place the topic on the public and political agenda, alerting stakeholders, such as politicians, NGOs, police, citizens and the press, to the disquieting state of the situation, and spurring them to develop both a policy and institutions to foster stakeholder collaboration. This includes related areas, such as rape, human trafficking and sexual violence that exacerbate intimate partner violence and femicide. Women's and other shelters (*krisesentre*) are reporting

---

[29] See *Dinutvei.no - nasjonal veiviser ved vold og overgrep håndbok for helsepersonell ved mistanke om fysisk mishandling (NKVTS)*: https://dinutvei.no

[30] See Justis- og politidepartementet (2000) *Handlingsplan om vold mot kvinner* (2000–2003); Justis- og politidepartementet (2007) *Handlingsplan mot vold i nære relasjoner «Vendepunkt» (2007-2011)*; Justis- og beredskapsdepartementet (2012) *Handlingsplan mot vold i nære relasjoner 2012, Meld. St. 15 (2012–2013)*; Melding til Stortinget, *Forebygging og bekjempelse av vold i nære relasjoner. Det handler om å leve. Regjeringens handlingsplan mot vold i nære relasjoner*, Vendepunkt 2008–2011.

an increased demand and a greater mixture of clients.[31] In relation to human trafficking, Norway reports to the European organization GRETA.[32] It calls for improved coordination; the training of relevant professionals; annual meetings between relevant authorities and NGOs; a new curriculum and special training for the police; the continued, regular updating of the knowledge base for the police; data collection and research; as well as assistance measures for child and adult victims of trafficking.

18. Poland (by Magdalena Grzyb)

18.1 Definition

The notion of femicide has lately been introduced into academic discourse in Poland (Grzyb, 2014), although its circulation is rather scarce.[33] The only context where the term is currently used is in media coverage of femicide in Latin American countries, especially in Central America and Ciudad Juarez, Mexico.

18.2 Resources

There is no institution, public or nongovernmental body that collects data on femicide. The official criminal statistics collected by the police on homicides have disaggregated data according to the victim's sex since 2016, although these statistics are not published, and it is therefore impossible to establish whether

---

[31] See Amnesty International Norge (2008) *Rapport om vold mot kvinner i asylmottak i Norge*, Oslo: Amnesty International, Norge; *Krisesentersekretariatets innspill (2012) Innspill til St. meld om menns vold mot kvinner og vold i nære relasjoner. Det handler om å leve.*

[32] See *Action against Trafficking in Human Beings*, 2005, www.coe.int/en/web/anti-human-trafficking/home

[33] Grzyb (2014) proposed a broader definition of femicide as the killing of a woman because of her gender (not necessarily by a man).

a female victim was killed by a male or female perpetrator, or the nature of the relationship between them. Therefore, these cannot serve as a source of precise information on femicide. It can be averred that there are no reliable empirical research studies on femicide in Poland.

19. Portugal (by Sofia Neves)
19.1 Definition

Intimate partner violence is addressed as part of the autonomous crime of domestic violence, under Article 152 of the Portuguese Penal Code:

> Whoever, in a repetitive manner or not, imposes physical or mental abuse, including bodily punishment, deprivation of liberty and sexual offences upon the spouse or ex-spouse; upon a person of another or of the same sex with whom the perpetrator maintains or has maintained a relationship equivalent to a spousal relationship, even if without cohabitation; upon a progenitor of a common descendant in the first degree; or upon a person particularly undefended, due to age, deficiency, disease, pregnancy, or economic dependency, who cohabits with him, shall be punishable by sentence of imprisonment from one to five years. If the agent commits the act against a minor, in the presence of a minor, in the common domicile, or in the victim's domicile, he shall be punishable by sentence of imprisonment from two to five years. If death results from the acts referred to above, the perpetrator shall be punishable by sentence of imprisonment from three to ten years and in the cases where it results in grievous bodily injury, the agent is punished with sentence of imprisonment from two to eight years.

Portugal remains embedded in conservative and patriarchal cultural values about family and intimacy, which favour the social acceptance of gender inequality, particularly in the family context. The designation of femicide has not been adopted by the current Portuguese administration and is relatively unused in general. The terms most used are 'homicide' or 'marital homicide'.

19.2 Resources

Despite the extensive nature of the phenomena and the legal advances made in the last decades (Lourenço et al, 1997), Portugal does not have a specific national legal and regulatory framework concerning data collection on VAW. Both the Ministry of Justice and the Ministry of Internal Administration collect data on marital homicide. Beyond criminal statistics, provided by official administrative sources, data collection on marital violence is conducted mainly by academics and civil society organizations, particularly women's associations, with each entity adopting different approaches and methods.

Since 2008, the Ministry of Internal Administration has issued a report on domestic violence annually, entitled *Domestic violence: Annual report of monitoring*, which integrates information concerning crime registrations, based on complaints reported to the policing authorities – the Republican National Guard (GNR) and the Public Security Police (PSP).

The Portuguese Observatory of Murdered Women – a mechanism created in 2004 by the Women's Collective Alternative and Answer (UMAR) – produces periodical reports on femicide. The Portuguese Association for Victim Support (APAV) recently created a Homicide Crimes Observatory, where marital homicide crimes are also analysed.

In 2016 the Portuguese government created the Team for Retrospective Analysis on Domestic Violence Homicides (Ordinance No. 280/2016, October 26), whose mission is to conduct a retrospective analysis of homicide situations that occurred in the context of domestic violence, with a view to developing preventative measures (Lisboa et al, 2005, 2006, 2008, 2009; Neves and Nogueira, 2010; Pais, 2010; Almeida, 2012; Matos, 2013; Pereira et al, 2013; Neves, 2016; Neves et al, 2016; UMAR, 2016).

20. Romania (by Ecaterina Balica)
20.1 Definition

In Romania, the concept of femicide first appeared in 2014 (Balica et al., 2014). From then onwards, there have been a number of studies focused on femicide-suicides (Balica, 2016), femicide (Balica, 2017), femicide between Romanian immigrant communities (Balica, 2018b) and young intimate femicide (Balica, 2018a). This term is utilized only in academic papers. In these studies, femicide is defined by the Romanian researcher as "the killing of a woman by an intimate partner". Partner is defined in a broad sense, to include a husband, living and dating partner, or lover; a former husband, former partner and former lover are also included in the definition.

20.2 Resources

Only one institution that has collected femicide data in Romania: the Laboratory Violence and Crime, Mediation and Prevention of the Institute of Sociology of the Romanian Academy (whose coordinator is C. Balica). Since 2015, Balica has initiated a pilot project to collect information about femicide committed in Romania between 2011 and 2015. To date, the database contains information from online media for about 298 cases of femicide committed in Romania. The definition of femicide used for this database was as follows: "femicide is best defined as the intentional killing of a woman by an intimate partner". The femicide in Romania database (n=298 cases) includes information about victims, aggressors and violence.

21. Serbia (by Ljiljana Stevkovic and Vesna Nikolic-Ristanovic)
21.1 Definition

In Serbia, femicide as form of gender-based homicide has been introduced as a concept over the course of the past decade by feminist academics and activists. The general definition of this term is relatively narrow, and it is only applied to killings of women in the family and partner context (Jaric, 2015). However, it has not been yet recognized as a term in official documents (such as the Criminal Code), or in official communications concerning gender-based violence. The term 'killing of women', which is in use, includes intimate partner homicide, usually following a period of continuous violence.

Although the term femicide is not in official use, the killing of women in the family/partner context has been recognized in several articles of the Criminal Code:[34]

1. Article 114: 'the killing of a family member whom the perpetrator had previously abused' as aggravated homicide. Although it is not specified, this type of homicide includes the killing of a woman by her intimate partner.
2. Article 121a: the death of women as consequence of genital mutilation.
3. Article 194, para. 4: the death of a family member (including a current or former intimate female partner, although not specified), as a consequence of family violence. The difference between this type of homicide and the act incriminated under

---

[34] See Criminal Code, Official Gazette of Republic of Serbia no. 85/2005, 88/2005, 107/2005, 72/2009, 111/2009, 121/2012, 104/2013, 108/2014, 94/2016.

Article 114 arises from the fact that the death of the family member is a consequence of the perpetrator's negligence.

In the past year, femicide has been covered extensively by the media, in order to raise awareness of the problem.

21.2 Resources

Two bodies currently collect data on femicide in Serbia:

1. Since 2010, the Women Against Violence Network (WAV Network) has collected and published statements and quantitative narrative reports on femicide, including data on victims, perpetrators, their relationship, what preceded the murder and the modus operandi of homicide (use of a weapon, whether the woman was beaten to death, strangled and so on), as well as analysis of media reports on femicide. The most rceently published quantitative narrative report and statement on femicide in Serbia cover the period from January to June 2017.[35] Both reports and statements are based on media coverage of femicide, since no official data exist for this type of homicide. During 2016, the WAV Network began monitoring femicide trials. It also launched a petition to declare 18 May as the day of remembrance for women killed by male members of their family and women victims of femicide.[36] The Serbian government approved the petition and declared 18 May as National Remembrance Day for

---

[35] See 'Femicid u Srbiji: 01. Januar – 30. jun 2017', www.zeneprotivnasilja. net/images/pdf/FEMICID_Saopstenje_01.januar-30.jun_2017.pdf; *Femicid: Ubistva žena u Srbiji, Kvantitativno-narativni izveštaj za 2017. godinu*, www.zeneprotivnasilja.net/images/pdf/FEMICID_Kvantitativno-narativni_izvestaj_01.januar-30.jun_2017.pdf; www.zeneprotivnasilja.net/ en/femicide-in-serbia

[36] The date was chosen in memory of seven women killed by their partners and male family members in 72 hours, on 15, 16 and 17 May in 2015.

all the victims of femicide. In 2017, the WAV Network organized an international conference entitled 'Femicide: Every murder of a woman is the responsibility and shame of the perpetrator, state and society', at which representatives of the Victimology Society of Serbia participated, as well as representatives of other national and international women's organizations.[37]

2. The Counselling Office Against Family Violence (COAFV) (Safe House) is an NGO, established in Belgrade in 1996, with the aim of helping women and children who are victims of family violence. COAFV holds records about women who have been murdered, with their photographs and basic information about the perpetrator, details of what preceded the murder and its modus operandi (use of a weapon in the killing, strangulation and so on) for 2011–14 (available only in Serbian).[38]

3. After a case of mass homicide, in which the primary victim was a woman killed by her former husband, the Ombudsman for Serbia carried out an inspection of the legality of the work of 45 centres for social work (CSW) operating in Serbia under the auspices of the Ministry of Internal Affairs and the Ministry of Labour, Employment and Social Issues.[39] The inspection revealed shortcomings in the work of official services and institutions, and resulted in recommendations for the improvement of work within the police, CSWs and health institutions, as well as recommendations for the improved implementation of international agreements.

4. A number of academic articles on femicide have been published in Serbian journals (see, for example, Mršević, 2013a, 2013b, 2014a, 2014b), and the journal *Temida*

---

[37] See www.zeneprotivnasilja.net/en

[38] See www.sigurnakuca.net/nasilje_nad_zenama/femicid/femicid_price_o_ubijenim_zenama.318.html?page=0&year

[39] See www.ombudsman.org.rs

published a special issue on femicide in 2016 (Batričević, 2016; Pavićević et al, 2016).

22. Slovenia (by Milica Antić Gaber and Jasna Podreka)

22.1 Definition

In Slovenia the concept of femicide is not in common use and is not recognized as an expression denoting the homicide of women. Moreover, it is not even currently employed in academic circles; nor does it appear in the media and, consequently, is not heard among the general population. The concept of femicide is utilized by only a few feminist scholars and researchers, and a number of NGOs working with women victims of violence. The problem of femicide is still underestimated and underresearched in Slovenia.

Is difficult to predict what the definition of femicide in Slovenia might be, because there is no public debate on the issue. In general, when someone uses the concept of femicide, he/she is referring to the killing of women by an intimate partner. However, in the academic field, we employ Russell's definition: 'the killing of females by males because they are females' (Radford and Russell, 1992). This definition is used to emphasize the term's political significance.

22.2 Resources

In Slovenia there is only one official body that can provide data on femicides, namely, the Ministry of the Interior. The ministry systematically collects statistical data about homicides of women, and considers the relationship between the victim and the offender to be key information.

Another important source on femicide in Slovenia is the first and only study on intimate partner femicide, conducted for PhD research at the Faculty of Arts and Science in Ljubljana, entitled 'Violence against women and intimate partner homicides of women in Slovenia' (Podreka, 2013). The report is based on the review and qualitative analysis of 24 criminal records from all the district courts in Slovenia, for the period 2000–11.

23. Spain (by Santiago Boira Sarto, Chaime Marcuello, Yolanda Rodriguez Castro, Maria Lameiras Fernandez, Laura Otero Garcia, Belén Sanz Barbero, Carmen Vives Cases and Isabel Goicolea Julian)

23.1. Definition

The 2004 Organic Law for Integral Protection against Gender-based Violence (GBV) (Law 1/2004) applies only to 'violence that men exert against women who are or have been their intimate partners, or who are or have been in an intimate relationship with them, with or without cohabitation'. The Spanish Penal Code specifies several crimes related to violence against women in the case of sexual crimes. The Penal Code increases penalties when the crime is committed under conditions that are specified as GBV. Article 153 of the Penal Code specifies the crime of injury in relation to GBV. However, Spanish legislation does not specifically stipulate femicide as a crime, and homicides and murders of women are included within Title 1 of the Penal Code, which deals with homicide in all its forms.

The restrictive approach to GBV in Spain, as framed in Law 1/2004, does not align with the definitions adopted by international organizations, such as the UN or the European Union. The restrictive approach to GBV under Spanish law prevents the affordance of visibility and development of intervention for other forms of GBV to which women in Spain are exposed, for example, murders of women in the context of prostitution, or murders of women when the perpetrator is not her current or former intimate partner. Official registers for such crimes do not exist in Spain.

The Spanish ratification of the Istanbul Convention implies that Spanish legislation needs to be amended accordingly.

However, to date, the official response – namely, the reform incorporated in the Organic Law 1/2015, 30 March, which modifies Organic Law 1/1995, 23 November, of the Penal Code – has been inadequate.

This reform includes the following amendments:

1. The addition of gender-based discrimination as an aggravating factor (Art. 22.4 of the Penal Code). Crimes against human life were modified to be considered aggravated crime in cases where homicide is committed after sexual aggression (Art. 172 bis).
2. The harassment (Art. 172 ter) and sharing, without the consent of the victim, of images taken in private locations with the victim's consent (Art. 197.7 of the Penal Code). Spanish legislation fails, as yet, to incorporate into the definition of GBV those cases where the aggressor is not a current or former intimate partner. This limitation was highlighted in the CEDAW report of 24 July 2015, which emphasized the need to include other types of GBV, such as: caretaker violence, police violence, or violence in public spaces, workplaces and schools . Although the term femicide is employed by certain social and academic institutions, its use is not generalized and it is utilized mainly in relation to the murder of women occurring within intimate relationships. In 2014, the 23rd edition of the Real Academia Española Spanish Language Dictionary incorporated the word *feminicidio*, defined as 'the murder of a woman due to her sex'.[40]

---

[40] See http://dle.rae.es/?id=Hjt6Vqr

23.2 Resources[41]

Since 2003, the statistical web of the Government Delegation for GBV at the Ministry of Health, Social Services and Equality has incorporated information on deaths due to GBV. In addition, the following information is available about deaths of women over the age of 15, aggregated by year:

- in relation to the victim: the complainant's characteristics, protective orders issued, violations of restrictive orders, country of birth, age, cohabitation with the aggressor, geographical location;
- in relation to the aggressor: country of birth, age, whether suicide was committed.[42]

Data compiled for the period 2003–05 emanated from Spanish media sources. Since 2005, the data have come from state law enforcement and security forces or from local police, and are corroborated by information provided by the judiciary. The statistics provide information on the sociodemographic characteristics of the victims (age, country of birth, relationship to the aggressor, cohabitation, geographic area, protection measures, police complaints and status of protection orders) as well as the characteristics of aggressors (country of birth, age and suicide). Recently, a statistical database that facilitates access to this information has been made available to the public (although access to individual data on homicides is not made public) under the title Portal Estadístico de la Delegación del Gobierno para la Violencia de Género (Statistical Portal of the Government Delegation for Gender Violence).[43]

---

[41] The following information is taken from Vives-Cases and Sanz-Barbero (2017).

[42] See www.violenciagenero.msssi.gob.es/violenciaEnCifras/victimasMortales/home.htm

[43] See http://estadisticasviolenciagenero.msssi.gob.es

Since 2007, the State Observatory on Violence Against Women, under the auspices of the Ministry of Health, Social Services and Equality, has published an annual report including information about all fatality victims of GBV. The latest report published includes information about murders committed in 2013 of women above the age of 15.

The General Council of Judicial Power (CGPJ) publishes data annually on VAW as part of judicial statistics where homicide crimes are reported.[44] Since 2007, the Observatory on Domestic and Gender-based Violence of the CGPJ, created in 2007, has published an annual report on death of victims due to domestic violence and GBV within intimate relationships. The latest report includes information about murders of women over the age of 15 committed in 2013.[45] It is important to note that these reports have been employing the term femicide since 2009, when referring to 'the violent death of a woman by her current or former partner, or a person who is or has been related to her by a similar affective relationship, and where the aggressor is a man'.

Some nongovernmental organizations also gather statistics on the number of women murdered, mainly by their intimate partners or ex-partners. It is important to mention in this context the Federation of Associations of Divorced and Separated Women, which facilitates access to media news published by the Spanish press in relation to femicide cases, from 1999 to today.[46] Additionally, the Fundación Mujeres feminicidio.net offers information on femicides committed in Spain, in any form, not limited to intimate partner femicide.[47]

---

[44] See www.poderjudicial.es/cgpj/es/Temas/Violencia-domestica-y-de-genero/Actividad-del-Observatorio/Datos-estadisticos/?filtroAnio=2015

[45] See www.poderjudicial.es/cgpj/es/Temas/Violencia-domestica-y-de-genero/Actividad-del-Observatorio/Informes-de-violencia-domestica

[46] See www.separadasydivorciadas.org/wordpress/estadisticas

[47] See www.feminicidio.net/menu-feminicidio-informes-y-cifras

The National Statistics Institute collects data related to mortality according to cause of death that is disaggregated by gender: the Instituto Nacional de Estadística (INE) *Estadística de defunciones según la causa de muerte*. Using these, it is possible to distinguish the most frequent causes of death among men and women.[48]

Cause of death is specified under the Index of International Classifications of Diseases (ICD), in which the classifications closest to the concept of femicide include 099 – aggressions (homicide, including a specific code for death related to abuse by a husband or partner); 100 – events of undetermined intention; and 102 – other external causes and later effects.

The INE also publishes statistics on homicides of women by their partner or ex–partner, based on information from the Government Delegation for Gender Violence.[49]

The General Council of the Judiciary, through the Observatory on Domestic and Gender-based Violence (created in 2002), compiles and analyses data obtained from legal statistics. This public institution produces an annual report on fatal injuries due to domestic violence.[50] Since 2004, this institution has used the term *feminicidio* and is the only public institution that currently does so. Since 2015, after the approval of Organic Law 8/2015, the deaths of minors at the hands of a father have also been considered direct victims of gender violence.

Another information source that compiles cases of femicide using a broader definition is the statistics webpage of the Federación de Asociaciones de Mujeres Separadas y Divorciadas (Federation of Associations of Separated and Divorced

---

[48] See http://ine.es/dyngs/INEbase/es/operacion.htm?c=Estadistica_C&cid=1 254736177008&menu=resultados&idp=1254735573002

[49] www.ine.es/ss/Satellite?L=es_ES&c=INESeccion_C&cid=125992614403 7&p=1254735110672&pagename=ProductosYServicios%2FPYSLayout

[50] See www.poderjudicial.es/cgpj/es/Temas/Violencia-domestica-y-de-genero/ Actividad-del-Observatorio/Informes-de-violencia-domestica

Women).[51] Information used to compile case files is sourced from notices published in the Spanish media. For each case registered, information is collected on the date of the event, the media outlet that obtained the information, the name and age of the victim, city and province, the relationship of the victim to the aggressor, and the notice published.

A newer initiative, feminicidio.net, publishes reports and statistics on femicide in Spain and Latin America. This is an initiative promoted by a feminist association that aims to afford visibility to cases not included in official.[52] Once again, media outlets provide the reference sources for information. Network reports provide data classified by the following parameters: year, location (autonomous community and province where the act occurred); age, occupation and country of origin of the victim; relationship to the aggressor; type of femicide (intimate or other types perpetrated by family members, death by robbery, prostitution, transphobia, inter alia); the existence of prior protective measures; and the available characteristics of the aggressor or about the act of violence.

Since 2003, the *Portal Estadístico de la Delegación del Gobierno para la Violencia de Género* (Statistical Portal of the Government Delegation for Gender Violence) of the Ministry of Health, Social Services and Equality of the Spanish Government has compiled the number of deaths due to violence perpetrated by a partner or ex-partner.[53] Using this information and data available via the National Statistics Institute on Female Homicide (CIE code 099), it can be shown that more than half of the cases of homicides of women are femicides due to gender violence.

---

[51] See www.separadasydivorciadas.org/wordpress/estadisticas

[52] See www.feminicidio.net/menu-feminicidio-informes-y-cifras

[53] See http://estadisticasviolenciagenero.msssi.gob.es

24. Sweden (by Lucas Gottzén and Sofia Strid)

24.1 Definition

The term femicide is not widely employed in Sweden. Swedish research on the matter is sparse, and the most common terms found are 'deadly violence', 'women killed by men', 'deadly intimate partner violence against women' and the gender-neutral 'deadly intimate partner violence' (Nybergh, 2016; Enander et al, 2017), which is also often used by government agencies (Brå, 2007; Kriminalvården, 2009; Polismyndigheten i Västra Götaland, 2013; Socialstyrelsen, 2014; SOU, 2015). Crime statistics and laws refer to 'deadly violence', which includes murder, manslaughter, child-slaughter and assault with deadly outcome (these are literal translations from Brå, 2016a), collectively termed 'deadly violence' (Brå, 2016a, 2016b). Common terms used by government agencies are 'deadly intimate partner violence against women' and 'deadly intimate partner violence' (see, for example, Brå, 2007; Socialstyrelsen, 2016), which refer primarily to the murder of a woman by an intimate partner. An intimate partner is commonly defined as a current or former husband, partner, boyfriend, girlfriend or lover, regardless of whether they were cohabiting at the time of the murder or had previously cohabited.

24.2 Resources

The main body that collects data on violent crime (including the murder of women and men) is the Swedish National Council for Crime Prevention (Brottsförebyggande rådet – Brå), an agency established in 1974, under the auspices of the Ministry of Justice. Brå is a centre for research and development within the judicial system, working primarily to reduce crime and improve levels of safety in society by producing data and disseminating knowledge on crime and crime prevention work. Brå produces Sweden's official crime statistics, evaluates reforms, conducts research to develop new knowledge and provides support to local crime prevention work. Brå's results form a basis for decision makers within the judicial system, parliament and the government. Brå often works in collaboration with other organizations and agencies in the public sector. It collects data on reported crime from the police, the customs authority, the public prosecutor and the courts. Other sources include Statistics Sweden (SCB), but the SCB statistics themselves draw on data from Brå.

Another, more qualitative, source is the National Board of Health and Welfare (Socialstyrelsen), a government agency under the auspices of the Ministry of Health and Social Affairs. This agency is required by law to conduct special investigations in cases where the cause of death is related to 'a crime conducted by a close, or formerly close person' (Socialstyrelsen, 2016). The aim of these investigations is to provide information that could be used in developing prevention measures in matters of intimate partner or family violence, as well as to enable long-term knowledge production. The National Board of Health and Welfare has been critical of its own investigations and has argued that it is impossible to draw any general conclusions, or make any systematic analyses, due to the sample being too small and too narrowly defined, and the fact that the board is not permitted to obtain information about the perpetrators.

25. Turkey (by Sümeyra Buran and Sadik Toprak)
25.1 Definition

There is insufficient concrete legal definition of femicide in Turkey. There has not yet been agreement as to the definition of femicide, as it can be confused with so-called 'honour killing' and 'revolt killing' in Turkey, but there are some related definitions around violence against women in Turkey (Yilmaz et al, 2015):

1. **Law No. 6284 on the Protection of Family and Prevention of Violence Against Women**: The purpose of the law is identified as 'regulating the principles and procedures as to the measures to be taken to protect and prevent violence against women and family members victimized by or under the risk of being subjected to violence, as well as the victims of stalking'. The law provides a definition of violence against women as follows: 'gender-based discrimination directed against a woman precisely because she is a woman, or that affects women disproportionately, and any attitude and behavior violating the human rights of women and defined as violence in this Law'. The Turkish Penal Code is the law that defines crime and punishment; and acts such as injury, killing, sexual assault and harassment, marital rape, menace and coercion are set forth as crimes within the Penal Code. Moreover, Violence Prevention and Monitoring Centres (VPMC) are being established under the provisions of this law.[54]

2. **Working Group Committee on Femicide:** Since 2009, the Ministry of Internal Affairs General Directorate of Security and the General Commandership of the Gendarmerie (Rural Police) have been using a 'Registration Form for Domestic Violence' and have therefore been recording data on femicide as a result of domestic violence committed against women expressly because they are women.[55] In 2017 a working group committee on femicide was established by the Ministry of Family and Social Policies, with the participation of representatives from the Ministry of Justice and the Ministry of Internal Affairs.

---

[54] See www.evicisiddet.adalet.gov.tr/en/dosya/up/icerik/1-6284-sayili-kanun.pdf

[55] See https://app1.jandarma.tsk.tr/KYSOP/uzaktan_egitim/Documents/4%20Jandarma.pdf

EXPLORING THE DATA ON FEMICIDE ACROSS EUROPE

3. **The National Action Plan on Combating Violence Against Women (2016–20)**: Violence against women is classified under four categories: physical, sexual, psychological and economic. Under Action 5.6, there is an action call defined as: 'analyzing incidents of violence against women resulting in death'.[56]

25.2 Resources

1. Turkey was one of the first signatories to the Council of Europe Convention on Preventing and Combating Violence Against Women and Domestic Violence (Istanbul Convention) on 11 May 2011. It was also the first country to ratify the convention, under Law No. 6284 on the Protection of Family and Prevention of Violence Against Women, prepared in accordance with the provisions of the Istanbul Convention, which entered into force on 20 March 2012.[57]

2. The Regulation on Opening and Operating Women's Shelters entered into force on 5 January 2013. As a result, 137 women's shelters were established with a total capacity of 3,433.

3. The Regulation on Violence Prevention and Monitoring Centres (ŞÖNİMs) entered into force following its publication in the *Official Gazette* on 17 March 2016. ŞÖNİMs provide consultancy, guidance and counselling services, and strengthening and supportive services, as well as monitoring services on a 24/7 basis and employing preferably

---

[56] See the definition of physical violence against women closely related to femicide: www.hips.hacettepe.edu.tr/ING_SUMMARY_REPORT_VAW_2014.pdf

[57] See Law on the Protection of Family and Prevention of Violence Against Women: www.ilo.org/wcmsp5/groups/public/---ed_protect/---protrav/---ilo_aids/documents/legaldocument/wcms_235174.pdf

female personnel.[58] First Step Stations were established in July 2011 and applied to ŞÖNİMs or to Family and Social Policies Provincial Directorates. These 'First Step Stations' service units function under the women's shelters which observe women victims of violence seeking shelter, examine their psychological and economic states and provide them with a place to stay for up to two weeks after their provisional acceptance.

4. Prime Ministerial Circular No. 2006/17 on 'Measures to be Taken towards Preventing Acts of Violence against Children and Women and Custom and Honour Killings' was published in 2006.

5. The ALO 183 Social Support Hotline operates 24/7 free of charge. It offers psychological, legal and financial counselling services for victims of violence or those at risk who need support.

6. The Pilot Scheme for the Electronic Support System was launched in 2012, whereby panic button devices (safety buttons) are given to women by the Violence Prevention and Watch Centres within the framework of a pilot scheme.

7. The General Directorate of Criminal Registration and Statistics, under the auspices of the Ministry of Justice, can collect data about female victims, women killings and honour killings, from the National Judiciary Informatics System (UYAP). However, specific femicide statistics cannot be downloaded from UYAP because of the lack of an article about femicide in 5237 Turkish Criminal Code, Article 82 (Qualified form of felonious homicide). The Ministry of Justice has started a new project about femicide, called 'offense–victim match', for UYAP, and this new data entry system is currently under construction.[59]

---

[58] See https://kadininstatusu.aile.gov.tr/uploads/pages/dagitimda-olan-yayinlar/the-violence-prevention-and-monitoring-centers-sonim-ingilizce.pdf

[59] See www.adlisicil.adalet.gov.tr/istatistik_2015/adalet2015/index.html#/0

8. The public institutions which provide active and direct data about femicide in provincial centers of Turkey are: The Domestic Violence Crimes Inquiry Offices (under the Office for Public Prosecution); The Departments of Combatting Domestic Violence and Violence Against Women at the Branch Offices of Public Security in 81 Provincial Directories of Security Child and Women's Section; and The Chief's Office at Provincial Gendarmerie Command. [60]

9. There are several studies on femicide originating from the Turkish medical community, focused mainly on pregnant or infertile women (Ergönen et al, 2008: 125–129; Yildizhan et al, 2009). However, the majority of studies were conducted by forensic pathologists who exposed femicide as part of their daily practice. One such study showed that the most common perpetrator was the husband or ex-husband (Karbeyaz et al, 2013). Another study pointed out that victims were mostly between the ages of 21 and 40 years, that firearms and strangulation were the most common causes of death, and that more than half of femicide cases can be classified as intimate partner violence (Unal et al, 2016). One study analysing domestic violence throughout Turkey demonstrated that domestic violence has a high prevalence and that reporting rates were lower in less developed regions (Toprak, 2016).

26. United Kingdom (by Hilary Fisher, Aisha K. Gill and Heidi Stöckl)
26.1 Definition

There is no agreed-upon UK government definition of femicide, and the term is not employed in official statistics.

---

[60] See Ministry of Internal Affairs General Directorate of Security and the General Commandership of the Gendarmerie (Rural Police): https://app1.jandarma.tsk.tr/KYSOP/uzaktan_egitim/Documents/4%20Jandarma.pdf; Turkish National Police Academy: https://www.pa.edu.tr/Default.aspx?page=Main&lang=En

26.2 Resources

The UK Home Office collects data on all homicides on the England and Wales Homicide Index, a computer-based system where all homicides are initially recorded by the police.[61] These data are categorized according to the sex of the victim. The motive in these statistics is not given based on the gender of the victim, but on the victim's relationship to the perpetrator. In Scotland, similar information is collected by the Scottish Government.

In the UK, the Femicide Census was developed by Karen Ingala Smith, CEO of Nia, in partnership with Women's Aid Federation England, and with support from Freshfields Bruckhaus Deringer and Deloitte LLP. For the work of the Femicide Census, femicide is defined as the killing of women by men, and is aligned to the earlier work of Diana Russell and Jill Radford, who defined femicide as 'the misogynistic killing of women by men' (Radford and Russell, 1992). The Femicide Census aims to provide a clear picture of femicide in the UK, in order to understand and address this phenomenon and, most importantly, to give a voice to the victims who have lost their lives to the most extreme manifestation of men's violence against women. It currently contains details on over 1,000 women killed by men in England, Wales and Northern Ireland since 2009. The Femicide Census database records the names of the women killed and their perpetrators, and it collects quantitative data disaggregated across age, occupation and health status, the elements of the killing itself – including the date, police area, weapon and recorded motive – as well as other available details for each case, relating to children, ethnicity and country of birth. The collection of this data demonstrates that these killings are not

---

[61] See www.ons.gov.uk/peoplepopulationandcommunity/crimeandjustice/ compendium/focusonviolentcrimeandsexualoffences/yearendingmarch2015/ chapter2homicide

isolated incidents and enables the analysis of trends and patterns in more depth, significantly furthering the understanding of the phenomenon of femicide. In her recent report to the General Assembly (A/71/398), the UN Special Rapporteur on violence against women specifically cites the UK's Femicide Census as an outstanding example of data collection practice.[62]

The underlying data for the Femicide Census was taken from Karen Ingala Smith's blog *Counting Dead Women*.[63] This information, as well as other publicly available information obtained primarily through online news articles, is verified and supplemented with information acquired from the police and other sources through Freedom of Information Act requests.

The first report from the Femicide Census was published in December 2016, drawing on findings from the 2009–15 cases (Femicide Census, 2016). This report received wide media coverage.[64] The report and the findings have been cited several times in the British Parliament, including during Prime Minister's Questions. Karen Ingala Smith and Women's Aid have showcased the census database and presented its findings to a wide range of audiences, including the OSCE Gender Section in Vienna, the Crown Prosecution Service and the College of

---

[62] See https://www.womensaid.org.uk/what-we-do/campaigning-and-influencing/femicide-census

[63] https://kareningalasmith.com/counting-dead-women/

[64] Media coverage of the first report included:
- *ITV*: www.itv.com/news/wales/2016-12-09/significant-rise-in-violence-against-women-in-2016-says-report
- *Telegraph*: www.telegraph.co.uk/women/life/900-women-have-killed-men-england-wales-past-6-years
- *New Statesman*: www.newstatesman.com/politics/feminism/2016/12/femicide-census-honours-victims-gender-violence
- *Reuters*: http://news.trust.org/item/20161207130106-19elh
- *Daily Mail*: www.dailymail.co.uk/wires/reuters/article-4009380/Male-partners-responsible-deaths-UK-women-killed-men--charities.html
- *Guardian*: https://www.theguardian.com/society/2016/dec/07/men-killed-900-women-six-years-england-wales-figures-show

Policing. A shorter report based on findings from data collated in 2016 was published in December 2017 (Femicide Census, 2017).

Conclusions

The main aim of this chapter was to present an overview of current femicide research across Europe, at both the global European and country level. To conclude, it is necessary to summarize weaknesses and strengths for the future.

Weaknesses

In most European countries, official statistics on femicide do not exist:

Annual crime reports issued by the police or national statistics agencies count annual cases of homicide or manslaughter; in many cases, but not all, they differentiate the gender of the victim and perpetrator. In some countries the statistics provide information on the victim–offender relationship; for the others, femicide is undetectable using the statistics. In countries where femicide or, at least, intimate partner homicide numbers or rates are available, many incidents lack complete information and data collection is discontinuous. The differences in national legal and reporting systems severely limit comparability across space and time. They also hinder appreciation of increases and decreases in femicide rates over time.

Data sources are extremely varied:

As the overview of resources in European countries shows, national or police statistics reports, court data, mortuary statistics and newspaper searches are the main sources of information. Each of these sources has advantages and disadvantages and should be carefully assessed before use. They work very well when used in combination: for example, newspaper searches provide detailed information (such as type and duration of victim–perpetrator relationship, weapon, location and more) and national statistics provide general quantitative information (rates, age cohorts, proportions across space, citizenship and so on) on the femicides. However, blending data while avoiding duplication of cases can be achieved only if the data can be matched, and this is usually not done, due to lack of coordination among the various institutional actors.

A common definition of femicide is lacking, as well as a legal definition:

The most common definition is of a 'woman intentionally killed by her former or current intimate partner'. However, this definition, which abounds in the media coverage of femicide, is rather narrow. It excludes the two ends of the age cohort: at one end, both unborn foetuses who are aborted because they are female and girls below the age of 16; at the other, older women who are killed by male relatives. Intimate partner femicide is a clearcut category, always including a sexual or gender-based dimension (Walby et al, 2017), yet femicide also occurs for other reasons.

Strengths

The most persuasive strength of femicide research in Europe is the abundance of initiatives, from grassroots data collection to official statistics:

The overview of resources for femicide research in European countries illustrates the multitude of ongoing small- and large-scale programmes in the different countries of Europe. Even if they are fragmented and sometimes disconnected, they constitute a very productive starting point for a European Observatory on Femicide, since interest, commitment, motivation and skill for femicide research abound in Europe.

There is dense interconnection between different actors that all play a part in analysing, preventing and combating femicide, or in protecting women's lives:

Government bodies, public and private research centres, NGOs, shelters, and activists have different tasks, but in order to collect robust and reliable data they need to relate to each other. The connection between governmental institutions and nongovernmental feminist actors working in the field of violence against women is still not an easy one in many countries; the power of the state has been both invoked and criticized by sociologists (Abraham and Tastsoglou, 2016; Corradi and Stöckl, 2016). Nevertheless, governments play an important role in intervention and prevention. An extensive analysis of femicide prevention, and how it is culturally shaped, is discussed in Chapters 4 and 5. However contested, this represents a necessary and very fruitful arena of cooperation between collective actors addressing violence against women. A renewed subjectivity has emerged for women's movements that will continue to develop through the engagement of open debate on the role and responsibility of the state to put an end to femicide and domestic violence.

References

Abraham, M. and Tastsoglou, E. (2016) 'Addressing domestic violence in Canada and the United States: The uneasy co-habitation of women and the state', *Current Sociology*, 64(4): 568–85.

Almeida, I. S. (2012) 'Avaliação de risco de femicídio: poder e controlo nas dinâmicas das relações íntimas' [Assessing the risk of femicide: power and control in the dynamics of intimate relations], unpublished PhD thesis, University of Lisbon, Portugal.

Asančaić, V. (2014) 'Femicid u kontekstu ukupnog nasilja i viktimizacije na štetu žena u Hrvatskoj u 21' [Femicide in the context of overall violence to and victimization of women in Croatia], PhD thesis, University of Zagreb, Croatia.

Attané, I., Brugeilles, C. and Rault, W. (eds) (2015) *Atlas mondial des femmes. Les paradoxes de l'emancipation* [*World Atlas of Women: The paradoxes of emancipation*], Paris: Editions Autrement.

Baldry, A. C. (2016) *Dai maltrattamenti all'omicidio. La valutazione del rischio per la prevenzione della recidiva e dell'uxoricidio* [*From domestic abuse to intimate homicide: Risk assessment for the prevention of recidivism and uxoricide*] (6th edn), Milan: Franco Angeli.

Baldry, A. C. and Ferraro E. (2008) *Uomini che uccidono. Cause, storie e investigazioni* [*Men who kill: Causes, histories and investigation*], Torino: Centro Scientifico Edizioni, Nuova edizione.

Baldry, A. C., Porcaro, C. and Ferraro E. (2011) 'Donne uccise e donne maltrattate. Stesso passato ma anche stesso destino?' [Murdered women and maltreated women: a similar past, but is their destiny also similar?], *Rassegna Italiana di Criminologia*, 4: 13–21.

Balica, E. (2016) *Homicide-Suicides in Romania: Statistical data and media representation*, Frankfurt: Peter Lang Publishing House.

Balica, E. (2017) 'Féminicide et médias en ligne. Études de cas: les femmes roumaines émigrantes qui offrent des services sexuelles légaux/illégaux' [Feminicide and the online media: case studies: Romanian émigré women offering legal / illegal sexual services], in V. Marinescu and S. Branea (eds) (2017) *Exploring political and gender relations: New digital and cultural environments,* Cambridge: Cambridge Scholars Publishing, pp 143–58.

Balica, E. (2018a) 'Young intimate femicide in Romania: incidence and risk factors', *Anthropological Researches and Studies* (in print).

Balica, E. (2018b) 'Femicidul în comunitățile de imigranți români' [Femicide within Romanian immigrant communities], *Revista Română de Sociologie*, 1(2): 83–99.

Balica, E., Branea, S. and Marinescu, V. (2014) 'Victimele violentei dintre partenerii intimi. Analiza datelor statistice privind victimele inregistrate in Romania, in intervalul 2008–2013' [Victims of intimate partner violence: analysis of Romanian cases between 2008–2013], Revista de Criminologie, Criminalistică și Penologie, 3/4: 24–34.

Batričević, A. (2016) 'Krivičnopravna reakcija na femicid' [The response to femicide in Criminal Law], *Temida*, 19(3–4): 431–52.

Brå (2007) *Utvecklingen av dödligt våld mot kvinnor i nära relationer* [*The development of deadly violence against women in intimate relationships*], Stockholm: Brottsförebyggande rådet.

Brå (2016a) 'Mord och dråp', www.bra.se/statistik/statistik-utifran-brottstyper/mord-och-drap.html

Brå (2016b) 'Fakta om våld i nära relationer', www.bra.se/statistik/statistik-utifran-brottstyper/vald-i-nara-relationer.html

Femicide Census (2016) 'Redefining an isolated incident, the Femicide Census Report for 2015', https://1q7dqy2unor827bqjls0c4rn-wpengine.netdna-ssl.com/wp-content/uploads/2017/01/The-Femicide-Census-Jan-2017.pdf

Femicide Census (2017) 'The Femicide Census: 2016 findings: Annual Report on cases of Femicide in 2016', www.womensaid.org.uk/what-we-do/campaigning-and-influencing/femicide-census/

Campbell, J. C., Webster, D., Koziol-McLain, J., Block, C., Campbell, D., Curry, M. A. et al (2003) 'Risk factors for femicide in abusive relationships: results from a multisite case control study', *American Journal of Public Health*, 93(7): 1089–97.

Corradi, C. and Piacenti, F. (2016) 'Analyzing femicide in Italy: overview of major findings and international comparisons', *Romanian Journal of Sociological Studies*, 1: 3–18.

Corradi, C. and Stöckl, H. (2014) 'Intimate partner homicide in 10 European countries: statistical data and policy development in a cross-national perspective', *European Journal of Criminology*, 11(5): 601–18.

Corradi, C. and Stöckl, H. (2016) 'The lessons of history: the role of the nation states and the EU in fighting violence against women in 10 European countries', *Current Sociology*, 64(4): 671–88.

EIGE (2014) *Administrative data sources on gender-based violence against women in the EU: Current status and potential for the collection of comparable data – technical analysis*, Luxembourg: Publications Office of the European Union, http://eige.europa.eu/sites/default/files/documents/MH0614061ENN.PDF

EIGE (2017) *Administrative data collection on rape, femicide and intimate partner violence in EU Member States*, http://eige.europa.eu/rdc/eige-publications/administrative-data-collection-rape-femicide-and-intimate-partner-violence-eu-member-states

Enander, V., Krantz, G., Lysell, H. and Örmon, K. (2017) *Dödligt våld i nära relation* [*Deadly Violence in Close/Intimate Relationships 2000-2016*], Gothenburg: Västra Götalandsregionen, www.nck.uu.se/digitalAssets/685/c_685348-l_3-k_enander-dodligt-vald-ppt-nationell-myndighetskonferens-viveka-enander.pdf

Ergönen, A., Ozdemir M. H., Can, I. O., Sönmez, E., Salaçin, S., Berberoğlu, E. and Demir, N. (2008) 'Domestic violence on pregnant women in Turkey', *Journal of Forensic and Legal Medicine*, 16(3): 125–9.

Eurostat (2016a) 'Database: crime and criminal justice', http://ec.europa.eu/eurostat/web/crime/database

Eurostat (2016b) 'Intentional homicide victims by age and sex: number and rate for the relevant sex and age groups', http://appsso.eurostat.ec.europa.eu/nui/show.do?dataset=crim_hom_vage&lang=en

Freysteinsdóttir, F. J. (2017) 'The different dynamics of femicide in a small Nordic welfare society', *Qualitative Sociology Review*, 13(3): 14–29.

Frye, V., Hosein, V., Waltermaurer, E., Blaney, S. And Wilt, S. (2005) 'Femicide in New York City: 1990 to 1999', *Homicide Studies*, 9(3): 204–28.

Granath, S., Hagstedt, J., Kivivuori, J., Lehti, M., Granpat, S., Liem, M. and Nieuwbeerta, P. (2011) Homicide in Finland, the Netherlands and Sweden: A first study on the European Homicide Monitor data, Stockholm: The Swedish National Council for Crime Prevention, the National Research Institute of Legal Policy, and the Institute for Criminal Law and Criminology at Leiden University.

Greuel, L. (2009) *Forschungsprojekt 'Gewalteskalation in Paarbeziehungen. Abschlussbericht'* [*Research project 'Increasing violence in partner relationship': Final report*], Institut für Polizei und Sicherheitsforschung (IPOS), https://polizei.nrw/sites/default/files/2016-11/Gewaltesk_Forschungsproj_lang.pdf

Grzyb, M. (2014) 'Kobietobójstw. Kryminologiczna charakterystyka zjawiska' [Femicide: a criminological approach], *Archiwum Kryminologii*, 36: 75–107.

Haller, B. (2014) 'Tötungsdelikte in Beziehungen. Verurteilungen in Österreich im Zeitraum 2008 bis 2010' [Murders in close relationships: sentences in Austria in the years 2008 to 2010], *SWS Rundschau*, H.1.: 59–77.

Hamel, C., Debauche, A., Brown, E., Lebugle, A., Lejbowicz, T., Mazuy, M. et al (2016) 'Rape and sexual assault in France: initial findings of the VIRAGE survey', *Population and Societies*, 538.

Heynen, S. and Zahradnik, F. (2017) *Innerfamiliäre Tötungsdelikte im Zusammenhang mit Beziehungskonflikten, Trennung beziehungsweise Scheidung. Konsequenzen für die Jugendhilfe* [Murders in the family in relation to conflicts, estrangement or divorce: Consequences for the wellbeing of young people], Weinheim: Beltz.

Holt, S. (2007) 'A matter of life and death: intimate partner homicide in Ireland', *Irish Journal of Family Law*, 10(4): 12–20.

Jaric, V. (2015) 'The UN-led interventions to prevent femicide in families and intimate partner relationships in Serbia (2010–2014)', in *Femicide volume III: Targeting of women in conflict*, Vienna: ACUNS, pp 130–38.

Jaspard, M. (2005) *Les violences contre les femmes* [Acts of violence against women], Paris: La Découverte.

Kapardis, A., Baldry, A. C. and Konstantinou, M. (2017) 'A qualitative study of intimated partner femicide and orphans in Cyprus', *Qualitative Sociology Review*, 13(3): 81–100.

Karbeyaz, K., Akkaya, H. and Balci Y. (2013) 'An analysis of the murder of women in a 10-year period in Eskişehir Province located in western Anatolia in Turkey', *Journal of Forensic and Legal Medicine*, 20(6): 736–9.

Kivivuori, J., Savolainen, J. and Danielsson, P. (2013) 'Theory and axplanation in contemporary European homicide research, in M. Liem and W. I. Pridemore (eds) *Handbook of European homicide research: Patterns, explanations and country studies*, New York: Springer, pp 95–109.

Knight, M., Tuffnell, D., Kenyon, S., Shakespeare, J., Gray, R. and Kurinczuk, J.(eds) (2015) *Saving lives, improving mothers' care: Surveillance of maternal deaths in the UK 2011–13 and lessons learned to inform maternity care from the UK and Ireland, Confidential Enquiries into Maternal Deaths and Morbidity 2009–13*, Oxford: MBRRACE-UK.

Kriminalvården (2009) *Män som dödar kvinnor de har barn med* [*Men who kill women they have children with*], Norrköping: Kriminalvårdens Utvecklingsenhet.

Kyriakidou, M. (2012) *Περιγραφικά Στοιχεία του Συνδέσμου Πρόληψης και Αντιμετώπισης Βίας στην Οικογένεια 1997-2012* [*Descriptive data of the Association for the Prevention and Handling of Violence in the Family 1997–2012*] (in Greek), https://docplayer. gr/12418735-Perigrafika-stoiheia-toy-syndesmoy-prolipsis-kai-antimetopisis-tis-vias-stin-oikogeneia-apo-to-1997-mehri-to-2012.html

Liem, M. (n.d.) *The European Homicide Monitor: How does it work and how may it benefit the understanding of femicide cases?* https://media. wix.com/ugd/61d2f3_6698b6ffe81a4bde9e7197daa93f6bd3.pdf

Liem, M., Ganpat, S., Granath, S., Hagstedt, J., Kivivuori, J., Lehti, M. et al (2013) 'Homicide in Finland, the Netherlands and Sweden: a first study on the European Homicide Monitor Data', *Homicide Studies*, 17(1): 75–95.

Lisboa, M., Vicente, L. and Barroso, Z. (2005) *Saúde e violência contra as mulheres: estudo sobre as relações existentes entre a saúde das mulheres e as várias dimensões de violência de que tenham sido vítimas* [*Health and violence against women: Study of existing relationships between women's health and various dimensions of violence experienced by victims*], Lisbon: Direcção-Geral da Saúde.

Lisboa, M., Carmo, I., Vicente, L., Nóvoa, A., Barros, P., Marques da Silva, S. et al (2006) *Prevenir ou remediar: Os custos sociais e económicos da violência contra as mulheres* [*Prevention or cure: Social and economic costs of violence against women*], Lisbon: Colibri.

Lisboa, M., Barros, P., Cerejo, S. D. and Barrenho, E.(2008) *Custos económicos da prestação de cuidados de saúde às vítimas de violência* [*Economic costs of healthcare provision for female victims of violence*], Lisbon: Direcção-Geral da Saúde.

Lisboa, Manuel, Barroso, Z., Patrício, J. and Leandro, A. (2009) *Violência e género: Inquérito nacional sobre a violência exercida contra mulheres e homens* [*Violence and gender: A national inquiry into violence exercised against women and men*], Lisbon: CIG.

Lourenço, N., Lisboa, M. and Pais, E. (1997) *Violência contra as mulheres* [*Violence against women*], Lisboan CIDM.

Marshall, I. H. and Summers D. (2013) 'Contemporary differences in rates and trends of homicide among European nations', in M. Liem and W. I. Pridemore (eds) *Handbook of European homicide research: Patterns, explanations, and country studies*, New York: Springer, pp 39–69.

Matos, S. P. (2013) 'Intimate femicide-suicide in Portugal', unpublished Master's thesis, University of Oporto, Portugal.

Mizrahi-Simon, S. (2016) *Spotlight: Violence against Women Report* (in Hebrew), Jerusalem: Israeli Knesset Research Institute, www.knesset.gov.il/mmm/data/pdf/m03643.pdf

Mouzos, J. (1999) 'Femicide: an overview of major findings', *Australian Institute of Criminology*, 124: 1–6.

Mršević, Z. (2013a) 'Ženoubistvo i samoubistvo ubice' [Killing of a woman and suicide by the killer], *Revija za kriminologiju i krivično pravo*, 51(3): 69–84.

Mršević, Z. (2013b) 'Femicid' [Femicide], *Pravo i politika*, 6(1): 51–69.

Mršević, Z. (2014a) 'Medijsko izveštavanje o femicidu' [Femicide in the media], *Temida*, 17(1): 81–96.

Mršević, Z. (2014b) *Nasilje i mi: Ka društvu bez nasilja* [*Violence and us: Towards a society without violence*], Belgrade: Institut društvenih nauka.

Neves, S. (2016) 'Femicídio: o fim da linha da violência de género' [Femicide: the end of the line for gender-based violence], *Ex-Aequo: Revista da Associação Portuguesa de Estudos sobre as Mulheres*, 34: 9–12.

Neves, S. and Nogueira, C. (2010) 'Deconstructing gendered discourses of love, power and violence in intimate relationships', in D. C. Jack and A. Ali (eds) *Silencing the self across cultures: Depression and gender in the social world*, Oxford: Oxford University Press, pp 241–61.

Neves, S., Gomes, S. and Martins, D. (2016) 'Narrativas mediáticas sobre o femicídio na intimidade: análise de um jornal popular português' [Media narratives about intimate femicide: analysis of a popular Portuguese newspaper], *Ex-Aequo: Revista da Associação Portuguesa de Estudos sobre as Mulheres*, 34: 77–92.

Nybergh, L. (2016) *Dödligt våld i nära relationer: En genomgång av internationell forskning* [*Lethal violence in close relationships: A review of international literature*], Gothenburg: Västra Götalandsregionen, http://nck.uu.se/kunskapsbanken/sokresultat-kunskapsbanken/?id=1293&librisId=&swepubId=

Pais, E. (2010) *Homicídio conjugal em Portugal. Rupturas violentas da conjugalidade* [*Conjugal homicide in Portugal: Violent breakdowns of conjugal relationships*], Lisbon: Hugin.

Pavićević, O., Glomazić, H. and Iljijić, Lj. (2016) 'Femicid kao deo kulture nasilja [Femicide as a part of a culture of violence], *Temida*, 19(3–4): 453–72.

Pereira, A., Vieira, N. and Magalhães, T. (2013) 'Fatal intimate partner violence against women in Portugal: a forensic medical national study', *Journal of Forensic Legal Medicine*, 20(8): 1099–1107.

Piacenti, F. and Pasquali, P. (2014) 'Femicide in Italy, between the years 2000–2012', *Rassegna Italiana di Criminologia*, 3, 181–92.

Podreka, J. (2013) *Nasilje nad ženskami in intimno partnerski umori žensk v Sloveniji* [*Violence against women and intimate partner homicides of women in Slovenia: doktorska disertacija*], Phd Thesis, Ljubljana.

Polismyndigheten i Västra Götaland (2013) *Polismyndighetens granskning av kvinnor som dödats av män i nära relation* [*The Police Authority's Examination of Women Killed by Men in Intimate Relationships*], Polismyndigheten i Västra Götaland.

Radford, J. and Russell, D. (1992) *Femicide: The politics of woman killing*, New York: Twayne.

Sela-Shayovitz, R. (2010a) 'The role of ethnicity and context: intimate femicide rates among social groups in Israeli society', *Violence Against Women*, 16: 1424–36.

Sela-Shayovitz, R. (2010b) 'External and internal terror: the effects of terrorist acts and economic changes on intimate femicide rates in Israel', *Feminist Criminology*, 5: 135–55.

Shalhoub-Kevorkian, N. and Daher-Nashif, S. (2013) 'Femicide and colonization: between the politics of exclusion and the culture of control', *Violence against Women*, 19(3): 295–315.

Šimonović, D. (2016) 'Violence against women, its causes and consequences: note by the Secretary-General', Report to the UN General Assembly A/71/398, www.un.org/ga/search/view_doc.asp?symbol=A/71/398&Submit=Search&Lang=E

Socialstyrelsen (2014) *Dödsfallsutredningar 2012–2013* [*Death Investigations*], Stockholm: Socialstyrelsen.

Socialstyrelsen (2016) *Dödsfallsutredningar 2014–2015: Barn och vuxna som avlidit med anledning av brott*, Stockholm: National Board of Health and Welfare, https://www.socialstyrelsen.se/Lists/Artikelkatalog/Attachments/20057/2016-1-31.pdf

SOU (Statens offentliga utredningar (2015) *Nationell strategi mot mäns våld mot kvinnor och hedersrelaterat våld och förtryck* [*National Strategy Against Men's Violence Against Women and Honour Related Violence and Oppression*], Stockholm: Fritzes.

Spinelli, B. (2008) *Femminicidio. Dalla denuncia sociale al riconoscimento giuridico internazionale* [*Femicide: From awareness-raising to international legal recognition*], Milan: Franco Angeli.

Stöckl, H., Devries, K., Rotstein, A., Abrahams, N., Campbell, J., Watts, C. and Garcia Moreno, C. (2013) 'The global prevalence of intimate partner homicide: a systematic review', *The Lancet*, 382: 859–86.

Stout, K. (1992) 'Intimate femicide: an ecological analysis', *Journal of Sociology and Social Welfare*, 29: 29–50.

Toprak, S. (2016) 'Domestic violence crimes between 2008–2011 in Turkey', *Cumhuriyet Medical Journal*, 38(4): 288–93.

UMAR (2016) *OMA – Observatório de Mulheres Assassinadas da UMAR: Dados 2015* [*UMAR Observatory of murdered women: 2015 data*], Lisbon: UMAR, www.umarfeminismos.org/images/stories/oma/2015/OMA_2015_Relat%C3%B3rio_Anual_Final.pdf

Unal, E. O., Koc, S., Unal, V., Akcan, R. and Javan, G. T. (2016) 'Violence against women: a series of autopsy studies from Istanbul, Turkey', *Journal of Forensic and Legal Medicine*, 40: 42–46.

United Nations (2014) 'Taking action against gender-related killing of women and girls', Resolution 68/191, adopted by the General Assembly on 18 December 2013.

United Nations Office of the High Commissioner for Human Rights (2015) 'UN rights expert calls all states to establish a "Femicide Watch"', https://www.ohchr.org/EN/NewsEvents/Pages/DisplayNews.aspx?NewsID=16796&LangID=E.%20A/71/398%2012/24%2016-16456

UNODC (2013) *Global study on homicide 2013: trends, contexts, data*, https://www.unodc.org/gsh

UNODC (2015) *International classification of crime for statistical purposes (ICCS): Version 1.0*, https://www.unodc.org/documents/data-and-analysis/statistics/crime/ICCS/ICCS_English_2016_web.pdf

Yildizhan, R., Adali, E., Kolusari, A., Kurdoglu, M., Yildizhan, B. and Sahin, G. (2009) 'Domestic violence against infertile women in a Turkish setting', *International Journal of Gynecology and Obstetrics*, 104(2): 110–112.

Yilmaz, E., Kumral, B., Canturk, N., Erkol, Z. and Okumus, A. M. (2015) 'Analysis and comparison of domestic femicide cases in the cities of Diyarbakir and Tekirdag, Turkey: a preliminary study', *Journal of Forensic and Legal Medicine*, 34: 17–23.

Vatnar, S.K.B. (2009) 'An interactional perspective on help-seeking women subjects to intimate partner violence', dissertation for PhD degree, Faculty of Medicine, University of Oslo.

Vatnar, S.K.B. (2015) *Partnerdrap i Norge 1990–2012. En mixed methods studie av risikofaktorer for partnerdrap* [*Murder of partners in Norway 1990–2012: A mixed methods study of risk factors in the murder of partners*], Oslo: Oslo Universitetssykehus.

Vives-Cases, C. and Sanz-Barbero, B. (2017) 'Femicide in Spain: data availability, opportunities and challenge', *Femicide*, 7: 56–62.

Walby, S., Towers, J., Balderston, S., Corradi, C., Francis, B., Heiskanen, M. et al (2017) *The concept and measurement of violence against women and men*, Bristol: Policy Press.

Weil, S. (2016) 'Failed femicides among migrant survivors', *Qualitative Sociology Review*, 12(4): 6–21, www.qualitativesociologyreview.org/ENG/archive_eng.php

Weil, S. (2017) 'Femicide of elderly women in Israel', in A. Filip and M. Platzer (eds) *Femicide Volume VIII: Abuse and femicide of the older woman*, Vienna: ACUNS, pp 32–3, http://acuns.org/wp-content/uploads/2017/11/Femicide-Volume-VIII-Abuse-and-Femicide-of-the-Older-Woman.pdf

SEVEN

Towards a European Observatory on Femicide

Shalva Weil and Marceline Naudi

Introduction

The definition of the term 'femicide' has been historically constructed and debated. Femicide is the culmination of different forms of violence against women and failure by the state to protect women from violence (WAVE, 2017b). As opposed to the 'homicide of women', or 'uxoricide', the term femicide is politically charged to bring awareness to the killing of women due to their gender. Often, but not always, these murders occur within societies structured on and functioning within deeply rooted patriarchal beliefs.

Today, women are still killed by their intimate partners. They are killed in the context of sexual crimes. Women are also targeted in armed conflict. Women die as a result of harmful practices such as female genital mutilation. Female foetuses are aborted, where preference for male offspring prevails. Women are killed in dowry-related crimes, as a result of organized crime or due to human trafficking, among others.

As we have seen in several chapters in this volume, in relatively recent years, various institutions and organizations in Europe and beyond have addressed the issue of femicide from the perspective of definitions, prevention, awareness raising, data collection and reporting. Efforts have taken place on national, European and international levels. The organizations involved in the work on femicide include the European Institute for Gender Equality (EIGE); the European network Women against Violence Europe (WAVE); the United Nations Special Rapporteur on violence against women, its causes and consequences; and Women's Aid England, among others. The work ranges from gathering information on Europe-wide availability of administrative data and compilation of definitions (EIGE, 2017a, 2017b); awareness raising and information sharing (WAVE, 2017a, 2017b), calling on states to collect and publish annual data on femicide, as well as to establish global, regional and national femicide and violence against women observatories (Šimonović, 2016); to establishing a national data system to collect information on women killed by men (Women's Aid, 2017).

The European Observatory on Femicide

As one of the aims of the COST Action IS1206, 'Femicide across Europe' (2013–17), a group of researchers and practitioners from 30 different countries committed themselves to setting up a European Observatory on Femicide. This was based on the development of new and innovative ideas, as well as taking stock of previous work in the area of femicide and building upon it, in order to effectively continue the prevention and combating of femicide in the future. Funded by the European Cooperation in Science and Technology (COST), the work of the Action involved discussions and decision making in the area of definitions, reporting, culture and prevention, and resulted in policy recommendations. The project culminated in an international Final Conference on Femicide, which took place at the University of Malta, 14–16 March 2017. The goal of the conference was to present the findings of the project as well as to commence work on establishing a European Observatory on Femicide, to be hosted initially at the University of Malta, within the Department of Gender Studies.

Establishing an Observatory on Femicide can be seen to respond to the call by the United Nations Special Rapporteur on Violence against Women to establish national and regional observatories on femicide, which will feed into a Global Femicide Watch. Marking the 16 days of Activism on 7 December 2017, Šimonović reiterated her call requesting states to intensify their efforts in this regard, and to publish every year, on the International Day on the Elimination of Violence against Women (25 November), the number of femicides under the categories of 'family or intimate partner-related femicides' and 'other femicides'.[1] The European Observatory represents a pioneering step in establishing in Europe a counting and reporting mechanism aimed at disseminating the much needed data and knowledge on femicide, with the ultimate goal of saving women's lives. As Šimonović stated, this will '… enable states to objectively assess where they stand on the regional and global scale and to adopt actions needed to prevent many preventable deaths of women'.

While the project of establishing an observatory contributes to the wellbeing of society, it is nonetheless an ambitious project for a variety of reasons, including the varied definitions of femicide across states, lack of funds, as well as limits to data comparability and quality. Nonetheless, it is a challenge worthy of addressing.

As with the establishment of any new, extensive and long-term project, the development of the observatory relies on past experience and data collection. In this case, it finds its basis in the results of the COST Action IS1206, 'Femicide

---

[1]   https://www.ohchr.org/EN/NewsEvents/Pages/DisplayNews.
aspx?NewsID=22510&LangID=E%20

across Europe'. One of the achievements of the Action is an agreement on how to proceed with the initial act of defining of femicide and a preliminary idea of how to filter femicide data. Most importantly, the Action resulted in a network of national researchers experienced in the field of femicide who are committed to the setting up the observatory.

The goals of the European Observatory on Femicide include monitoring, provision of data, advancing research, promoting comparability across states and gaining understanding of local contexts. Emphasis will also be placed on qualitative data (Weil, 2017; Weil and Kouta, 2017), which has been given insufficient attention to date by other observatories, NGOs and national institutions. Narratives of 'failed femicides' (Weil, 2016) may be of particular use in studying migrants in Europe and understanding cultural patterns. Liaison with a broad community of established organizations already engaged in the topic was started through a round table meeting with stakeholders held in Brussels in 2015 as part of the Action. This created opportunities for cooperation and support, and also widened the scope and outreach of the European Observatory on Femicide beyond Europe. Additionally, as we have seen, existing availability of some national statistics, qualitative data, single case studies, reports and articles provides a starting point for the European Observatory on Femicide, and should enable the collection of baseline data such as age, sex, relationship status, location and time.

Structure and the way forward

The European Observatory on Femicide has a scientific coordinator supported by a part-time researcher. They are supported by a steering committee,[2] country research groups,

---

[2] The scientific coordinator of the observatory is Marceline Naudi (University of Malta). She will be supported by a part-time research officer, Barbara

and organizations working in the field of preventing and combating femicide – all of whom have been connected and have shared their work thanks to the COST Action IS 1206, 'Femicide across Europe'. It is planned to have special interest hubs within the observatory, led by members of the steering committee, so as to enable past and ongoing work to be developed.

For the first two years (2018–19) the observatory will be based within the Department of Gender Studies at the University of Malta, which will be funding the part-time researcher. Part of the researcher's role will be to seek further funding for the future of the observatory.

The work has begun with setting up a coalition tasked with the establishment of the European Observatory on Femicide as a permanent endeavour, raising awareness of the urgent need for gathering comparable data across Europe; lobbying funders and institutions to allocate appropriate finances to the work on data collection on femicide; and lobbying Eurostat, the United Nations Office on Drugs and Crime (UNODC) and other national statistical agencies to disaggregate homicide data by gender of victim and perpetrator, and to provide data on the relationship between perpetrator and victim. Establishing the observatory to collect, analyse and review data at the regional level while facilitating the gathering of data at the national level will also galvanize the collection of information on good practices, enhancing the protection of women and girls from gender-based killings and violence.

Stelmaszek (University of Malta), and the steering committee: Anna C. Baldry (Università degli Studi della Campania 'Luigi Vanvitelli'), Santiago Boira Sarto (Universidad de Zaragoza), Consuelo Corradi (LUMSA University of Rome), Christiana Kouta (University of Cyprus), Maria J. Magalhães (University of Porto), Chaime Marcuello (Universidad de Zaragoza), Ksenia Meshkova (University of Erfurt), Monika Schröttle (TU Dortmund University) and Shalva Weil (Hebrew University of Jerusalem).

In order to establish a permanent European Observatory on Femicide, activities such as initial round table discussions to strengthen concepts and methodology, creating a virtual observatory via a website, and organizing visits to relevant institutions are planned. Work on solidifying the structure, mission statement and principles for the observatory, an annual working plan, methods of operation, desired outputs, and an overall strategy have already started. The observatory will be establishing country research groups tasked with feeding relevant data to the observatory. Existing national observatories on violence against women – such as those in Spain and Portugal, among others – with whom contacts have already been made through the COST Action, will be called upon to assist in the setting-up of the observatory and its work. Support will also be sought from Europe-wide organizations such as EIGE, UNODC, WAVE, the European Women's Lobby (EWL) and other NGOs such as Women's Aid England, which are already involved in the work in the area of femicide, and again, with whom the COST Action has already cooperated.

Conclusions

Establishing a European Observatory on Femicide is not about kudos. As Šimonović observed: 'Each case of femicide is an individual woman's tragic story and there is the urgent need to focus on the prevention of these avoidable killings by undertaking in-depth analysis aimed at identifying shortcomings in the criminal justice system'.[3] The CEDAW General Recommendation No. 35 and the Council of Europe Convention on Combating and Eliminating Violence against Women and Domestic Violence both recognize data collection

---

[3]   https://www.ohchr.org/EN/NewsEvents/Pages/DisplayNews.aspx?NewsID=22510&LangID=E%20

and its analysis as important tools to prevent gender-based violence against women.

It is therefore about bringing about change. It is about raising awareness of how the most basic of human rights – the right to life – is constantly being violated, on our watch and under our noses, with impunity. While gender-based violence against women has become more and more acknowledged, and steps continue to be taken to prevent and eradicate it, femicide, as its most extreme form, has garnered less acknowledgement. This must be changed. It is about time that we open our eyes to the devastation caused by femicide, not only to the women themselves, and their children and other relatives, but to society as a whole.

Our hope is that by publishing this book and collating the evidence from all over Europe, we can raise society's awareness of this heinous crime, so as to create a significant impact. Our hope is that as a result we can influence policies and legislation, so as to remove impunity and seek justice. Our expectation is that all those affected by the death of the women can find some solace in knowing that their narratives will prevent other women from dying. The ultimate aim is to prevent femicide. It is long overdue.

References

EIGE (2017a) *Administrative data collection on rape, femicide and intimate partner violence in EU Member States*, http://eige.europa.eu/rdc/ eige-publications/administrative-data-collection-rape-femicide- and-intimate-partner-violence-eu-member-states

EIGE (2017b) 'Gender Equality Index', http://eige.europa.eu/gender- equality-index/2015/countries-comparison/index/map

Šimonović, D. (2016) *Report of the Special Rapporteur on violence against women, its causes and consequences*, GA Res 69/147, UNGA, 71st Session, A/71/398.

Weil, S. (2016) 'Failed femicides among migrant survivors', *Qualitative Sociology Review*, 12(4): 6–21, www.qualitativesociologyreview.org/ENG/archive_eng.php

Weil, S. (2017) 'The advantages of qualitative research into femicide', *Qualitative Sociology Review*, 13(3), Special Issue: *Researching Femicide from a qualitative perspective*: 118–25, www.qualitativesociologyreview.org/ENG/Volume42/QSR_13_3.pdf

Weil, S. and Kouta, C. (2017) 'Femicide: a glance through qualitative lenses', *Qualitative Sociology Review*, 13(3), Special Issue: *Researching Femicide from a Qualitative Perspective*: 6–12, www.qualitativesociologyreview.org/ENG/Volume42/QSR_13_3_Weil_Kouta.pdf

Women against Violence Europe (WAVE) (Producer) (2017a) *Preventing and tackling femicide* [Webinar], www.youtube.com/watch?v=96MOnyAE10o&index=2&list=PLiySr0eGbRYakNzIw5-m3oSGEygNapxtY

Women against Violence Europe (WAVE) (2017b) 'WAVE thematic paper: preventing and eradicating femicide', http://fileserver.wave-network.org/researchreports/Thematic_Paper_Femicide_15Febr2017.pdf

Women's Aid (2017) *Femicide census: Profiles of women killed by men*, https://www.womensaid.org.uk/what-we-do/campaigning-and-influencing/femicide-census

Notes on contributors

Anna Costanza Baldry is a Full Professor at the Department of Psychology of the Università degli Studi della Campania Luigi Vanvitelli, Italy. She has been collaborating for over 20 years with NGOs and addressing risk assessment, femicide and orphans of femicide. She has published 100 articles in prestigious national and international scientific journals, book chapters and monographs, as well as presented her work at numerous national and international conferences. She has coordinated several prestigious projects with special emphasis on women victims of violence. She is a visiting scholar at the Institute of Criminology, Faculty of Law, University of Cambridge.

Santiago Boira graduated in Psychology from the University of Salamanca, Spain, and received his PhD from the University of Zaragoza, Spain. He is currently a Lecturer in the Department of Psychology and Sociology and a coordinator of the Master's degree in gender relations at the University of Zaragoza. His research interests focus on gender issues, intimate partner violence, especially in men abusers. He is a member of the network 'Femicide across Europe', Cost Action IS1206. He is also a researcher of the Group of Social and Economic Studies of the Third Sector (GESES).

Sümeyra Buran is an assistant professor of English Language and Literature at Social Sciences University of Ankara, Turkey. She is also a committee member in the Unit of Women Studies and Problems in Academia at the Council of Higher Education.

She is studying British Literature, British Science Fiction, British Women Writers, Women Studies, Academic Women, Social Gender Inequality, Gender Mainstreaming, Violence Against Women, Femicide, Science Fiction Literature, Cyber and Cyborg Literature, and TechnoFeminism. She has coined a new approach with her recent book *TechnoFeminist Science Fiction* (Addleton Academic Publishers, New York, 2015).

Aisha K. Gill, PhD, CBE is Professor of Criminology at University of Roehampton, UK. Her main areas of interest and research are health and criminal justice responses to violence against black, minority ethnic and refugee women in the UK, Iraqi Kurdistan and India. She has been involved in addressing the problem of violence against women and girls/'honour' crimes and forced marriage at the grassroots level for the past seventeen years. Her recent publications include articles on honour killings, femicide, coercion and forced marriage, child sexual exploitation and sexual abuse in South Asian communities, female genital mutilation and sex selective abortions.

Magdalena Grzyb is an Assistant Professor in the Criminology Department, Jagiellonian University in Kraków, Poland. She received her PhD from Jagiellonian University and Bordeaux University, France and authored a book *Culturally motivated crimes. Criminal justice responses to harmful traditional practices in Western democratic liberal states* (Wolters Kluwer Polska, 2016) published in Polish. Her research interests cover violence against women, femicide and intersections of feminism and penal populism.

Christiana Kouta is an Associate Professor at the Department of Nursing, Cyprus University of Technology. She is the Head of the Master in Advance Nursing and Community Health and Care. She is teaching Community Nursing, Health Promotion, Transcultural Nursing, Family Nursing. Dr Kouta's research combines community and transcultural health related to culture and gender. Currently, she is leading an EU funded project on knowledge platform for FGM. She is involved in other EU projects related to Cultural Competent and Compassionate Health Care. She is the scientific coordinator in the COST Action Femicide across Europe and the Secretary of the European Transcultural Nurses Association.

Maria José Magalhães is Full Professor at FPCEUP, researcher member of CIEG and CIIE. She received the Award Carolina Michaelis de Vasconcelos – Research on Women's Studies/1990. Her current main field of research is on gender violence and femicide, member and coordinator of several research projects. Currently, she is the Leader of the transnational Project 'Bystanders: developing bystanders' responses among young people', funded by EU REC Progamme. She was also the Principal Investigator (Portugal) of the transnational Project CEINAV, funded by HERA-ESF (2013–2016); MC member of the COST – Femicide Across Europe (2013-2017) and scientific Coordinator of the Observatory of Women Murdered, OMA-UMAR (2004–2010).

Chaime Marcuello-Servós is a lecturer in Social Work and Social Services in the Department of Psychology and Sociology at the University of Zaragoza, Spain; and a professor on the Inter-Doctoral Programme in Science and Humanities for Interdisciplinary Development at the CEICH of the UNAM and the UAdeC, Mexico. In addition, he is Coordinator of the Interdisciplinary Teaching Innovation Group (GIDID); and co-founder of the Third Sector Social and Economic Studies Group (GESES). He is President of the RC51 on Sociocybernetics (2014–2018) of ISA. He is Editor of *Current Sociology Monographs* and *SAGE Studies in International Sociology* (SSIS) Books (2016–2019) and co-director of the *Iberoamerican Journal of Development Studies*.

Ksenia Meshkova is a graduate of Saint Petersburg State University, Tartu University, Estonia, and Erfurt University, Germany. She is currently writing her PhD thesis titled 'Intimate Partner Violence in Modern Russia' at the Humboldt University in Berlin, Germany. Her studies have been sponsored by German Academic Exchange Service and Friedrich Ebert Foundation. Ksenia is an active member and young scholars' day organiser of the European Network on Gender Violence. Currently Ksenia is coordinating the 10th European Feminist Research Conference in Göttingen and teaching at the Protestant University of Applied Sciences in Berlin.

Anita Nudelman is an applied medical anthropologist, who lectures at the Faculty of Health Sciences, Ben Gurion University, Israel. Her areas of expertise include traditional healing, gender issues, sexual health and HIV. She has led community-based Rapid Assessment Processes in Africa (UNAIDS, the Global Fund), as well as gender and culture-sensitive comprehensive sexuality projects – including prevention of gender-based violence HIV. She participated in the COST Action IS1206 'Femicide across Europe' and is Co-Chair of the Committee on Anthropology and HIV/AIDS of the International Union of Anthropological and Ethnological Studies (IUAES).

Monika Schröttle is Professor at the Technical University of Dortmund, Germany, and is leading research projects for the Institute for Empirical Sociological Research in Nürnberg. She is an expert in violence against women and prevalence research, disability studies and empirical human rights research. She is coordinating the European Network on Gender and Violence (www.engv.org) with almost 400 researchers, and has been coordinating several working groups on data collection and monitoring of gender based violence in European research networks. In her last project she developed a 'Measurement framework on violence against women' for the Gender Equality Index of the European Institute for Gender Equality (EIGE).

Ljiljana Stevkovic is a PhD student and teaching assistant in the Faculty of Special Education and Rehabilitation at Belgrade University, Serbia. She is a member of the European society of criminology (ESC), the European working group of researchers on organised crime (EUROC) and the ESC victimology working group. She has participated in numerous projects regarding crime victims, juvenile delinquency and victims of domestic violence. In the area of her research interest Ljiljana has published numerous papers dealing with the problem of gender based violence, juvenile delinquency and victimisation of children and the elderly.

Index

References to figures and tables are in *italics*. References to notes have '*n*' after them.